Criminal Justice
Recent Scholarship

Edited by
Marilyn McShane and Frank P. Williams III

A Series from LFB Scholarly

Delinquency, Schools, and the Social Bond

Christine A. Eith

LFB Scholarly Publishing LLC
New York 2005

Library of Congress Cataloging-in-Publication Data

Eith, Christine A., 1975-
  Delinquency, schools, and the social bond / Christine A. Eith.
    p. cm. -- (Criminal justice : recent scholarship)
  Includes bibliographical references and index.
  ISBN 1-59332-093-0 (alk. paper)
  1. School environment--United States. 2. Socialization--United
States. 3. Juvenile delinquency--United States. I. Title. II. Series:
Criminal justice (LFB Scholarly Publishing LLC)
  LC210.5.E38 2005
  306.43'2--dc22

2005012789

ISBN 1-59332-093-0

Printed on acid-free 250-year-life paper.

Manufactured in the United States of America.

TABLE OF CONTENTS

LIST OF FIGURES AND TABLES

ACKNOWLEDGMENTS

This project, particularly at such a early stage in my career, is a one that is grounded in fantastic mentorship and collegial support. I was lucky enough to work with four wonderful women who helped advise and shape this research. I am grateful to Ronet Bachman, Susan Miller, Julie Hubbard, and in particular Cynthia Robbins who provided tireless support and skilled suggestion to help develop these ideas. I am also incredibly lucky to have colleagues such as Carol Gregory, Ken Lachlan, Brian Monahan, Michelle Meloy, Shana Maier and Christina Lanier who kept me smiling through this process. I wish to thank each of them for their assistance, tolerance, and friendship. While I have had the pleasure of working with wonderful scholars, Steve Cernkovich remains a role model of how to balance my own life in the word of academia. I am truly lucky and forever grateful for Steve's teachings, guidance, mentorship and seemingly undying support. I also owe an incredible debt of gratitude to Marty Schwartz whose guidance and suggestion gave me the direction to submit this manuscript. I further wish to thank Marylin McShane, Frank Williams, and Leo Balk for their comments, suggestions, editorial skill and especially patience through the formatting process.

It is also imperative to thank those who made this project possible by facilitating the data used in the analysis. In particular, I extend my gratitude to Steve Martin for access to a portion of the data used in this analysis, Roberta Gealt and Dan O'Connell who provided thoughts and suggestions regarding this project, Susan Silberman and Peter McCabe for introducing me to the Education and Secondary School Survey, and the Delaware Department of Education who generously and graciously fulfilled every request for data or information. This project was supported in part by data funded by Cooperative Agreement #SP08192 to Delaware's Division of Substance Abuse and Mental Health, Delaware Health and Social Services.

I also wish to thank Sr. Trinitas Bochini, Jon Stanton, Pat Kirby, Christy Harnett, and Sally Wall, and other colleagues at the College of Notre Dame of Maryland for their humor and patience. I would also like to thank Ciera Laury for her research assistance in the final revision of this book.

Finally, and most especially, I would like to thank my parents, family and friends who have always provided me with endless love and support. Words can never express my gratitude to each of you but, in this format, it's the best I can do. Thanks for everything.

Chapter 1

Public Schools and the Social Bond

Introduction

United States Public Schools face a number of complex issues in modern society. Schools are expected to provide youth with a safe learning environment in which they can gain a level of knowledge to make them productive members of society. In the wake of the tragic events at Columbine High School, the public has become fascinated and fearful of those extreme incidents of school violence. While these are statistically rare incidents in the United States, these acts of violence have increased the public's concern for the climate of public schools. One aspect of the school climate that has been in question is the bond a student has with his or her school. Specifically, the school bond is a fondness or affinity for the teachers, staff and administrators, and a pride in the school itself.

The importance of the school atmosphere and the student-school bond is grounded in sociological, school psychology, and education literature. Social control theory, as defined by Travis Hirschi, suggests that conforming behavior is a result of strong pro-social bonds with society. When a student has an attachment to the school, is committed to school and academic success, is involved in school related activities, and believes that the rules and policies of the school are fair, he or she is less likely to engage in delinquent activities. Researchers have focused on the school bond as a preventive factor in the study of delinquency, indicating that students who are less bonded to school are more likely to engage in delinquency. It can be argued, however, that the relationship between school bonding and delinquency is reciprocal. That is, a strong bond to school will reduce a student's likelihood of engaging in delinquent behavior, however, engaging in delinquent behavior should also reduce one's bond to school.

This research will look at the student-school bond relationship with delinquent behavior and the school environment, and how this differs across the transitions from elementary to middle and into high school. Specifically, this research will take a unique approach to the study of school bonding by concentrating on what individual and school level variables can predict the school bond. In addition, this study will assess how the models of school bonding change across the transitions from elementary to middle and into high school by testing models of school bonding on 5th, 8th, and 11th grade samples.

Schools perform an important role in shaping the norms, values and life chances of American youth. Education is no longer a privilege of the wealthy, rather a service that is guaranteed to all American citizens. Children have their first interaction with the educational system around the age of 5, and continue to maintain contact until around the age of 18. In total, youth in the United States will spend approximately 13 years of their life in the education system. Given the amount of time spent in the academic setting, aside from the family, the institution of education becomes the primary instrument of socialization for youth. In other words, the school is responsible for teaching not only substantive information, but also the norms and values of the society.

For certain students, however, the school environment is not a comfortable atmosphere Public schools follow the norms and values of the middle class, specifically delayed gratification and the value of educational achievement. Students who come from homes where these middle class values are not reinforced tend to experience dissonance and struggle to behave in the socially appropriate way dictated by the school, thus reducing their bond to the school. In addition, as these students struggle to adhere to the rules of the school, they are often chastised or reprimanded for their inappropriate behavior.

Whereas it is the prerogative of the parent to discipline a child's negative behaviors in the home, when children do not follow the rules in school, their discipline is left to the discretion of school officials. The school rules, much like those of society, are designed to be uniformly enforced across all members of the school. However, as previously discussed, school disciplinary efforts may inadvertently target those students who come from diverse backgrounds and do not share the middle class experience. Thus, the conflict stemming from an unfair disciplinary system may lead to a reduction in the student-school bond.

In addition to discipline, other school factors may influence the student-school bond. School enrollment is suspected of influencing the school bond. Those schools with a large student body will have a lower mean level of school bonding. There are rarely enough teachers and school officials to monitor the behavior of all students at all times. Moreover, there is a lack of attachment found between teachers and students. The school environment is also impacted by the students who comprise it. Schools are comprised of a diverse group of students, and without the appropriate guidance from teachers and school officials, diversity may lead to a reduction in school bonding among students. If minority students can not find a group of similar peers, or if the school environment conflicts with the norms and values present in their home, the students may be less bonded to the school.

Schools are a social institution much like the family, reinforcing pro-social norms and values while punishing antisocial behavior. As such, it could be assumed that individuals can develop a connectedness to the school as one would to their family. This connectedness, or bond, may not take the same form as a familial bond, but nevertheless works as a protective factor in preventing antisocial or delinquent behaviors.

While researchers have attempted to explain the relationship between delinquency and school bonds, few have focused on what influences a student's bond to school. Sociological research suggests that a strong bond to school is a protective factor against delinquency, however, there is little sociological research focused on the protective or risk factors associated with a strong school bond.

In addition, little previous research has addressed the school environment when studying school bonds. While education research has recognized the importance of the hierarchical data structure present in school research, sociologists have rarely addressed such issues. It is difficult to assess the direct impact of the school environment on the student-school bond; however, sociological research has ignored the explanatory power of the between school variation on the study of school bonds.

This research examines student-school bonds in three grades, 5th grade, 8th grade, and 11th grade. Figure 1, on page 9, illustrates a very general conceptual model for directionality. This project will look at how individual level factors such as race and gender, academic achievement, and measures of individual and peer delinquency influence an individual's social bond to his or her school. Further, this project will analyze the impacts that other school-level factors such as size, school poverty, use of ability grouping, minority enrollment, average rate of delinquency among students, and discipline that is imposed by the school have on the individual school bond across schools.

This study will provide a model of school bonding that accounts not only for individual factors relating to the school bond but also simultaneously model the impact that the school environment will have on such a bond. This will provide readers with an understanding of the complex relationship between the individual and the school environment, particularly how certain school factors can impact the relationship of specific individual characteristics moderating the school bond. It is an important void to fill in the sociological literature which has neglected to address the hierarchical structure of school data in the study of school bonding. In addition, policy implications will be informed by the results to help students and schools create strong and healthy bonds through social interventions and policy changes. The goal of these policy recommendations is also to guide practitioners and school administration on potentially effective measures they can take to improve the student-school bonds at their institution.

The following pages will provide the reader with a theoretical context which leads to the study of school bonds. Chapter 1 continues with an assessment of the theoretical perspective as well as a review of the literature that has been conducted on the topic of school bonding. Chapter 2 lays out the hypotheses for this project as well as a description of the data, variables and statistical analysis used for this study. The results of the analysis will be presented in Chapters 3 to 5, and finally Chapter 6 provides conclusions that can be drawn from the results and potential policy implications that can assist students and schools to forge strong and beneficial bonds.

Figure 1: General Conceptual Model for the Directionality of Predicting School Bonding.

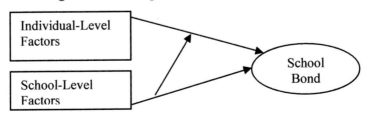

Theoretical Perspective

Criminologists have developed many theories to describe why people do not uphold the rules of their social environment. Travis Hirschi (1969) took a new approach to this age old question. Instead of asking why people violate the rules of society, he chose to ask why individuals conform to the rules of society. To answer this question, Hirschi offered a social control theory which described four social controls that sustain our desire for conformity.

Travis Hirschi proposed that delinquency is a result of weakened or broken bonds to society. He proposed that there are four elements to a social bond; attachment, commitment, involvement, and belief. Each of these elements is highly correlated with the others and as such, when one element is weakened it will result in the weakening of the others (Akers, 1997). Hirschi contends that if all of the elements of the social bond are intact, then the child will conform to the rules of society. However, if one or more of the elements of the social bond is weakened or missing, delinquency will result. Hirschi proposed that individuals develop different types of bonds with society, including those to family, peers, and school. Certain bonds may become stronger protective factors during different periods of life. In the case of school aged children, school factors have been found to be consistently stronger protective factors than even ties to family (Crosnoe, Erickson, & Dornbusch, 2002). Social control theory, as defined by Hirschi (1969), was one of the first theories which dealt with the development of school bonding and identified the lack of school bonds as a primary cause of delinquency (Maddox & Prinz, 2003).[1]

Attachment to School

Attachment addresses the connection an individual has with others. If an individual has respect for, cares about, and/or identifies with others he or she will then care about their expectations. This is the component that Hirschi contends is the "sociological counterpart to the superego or conscience" (Hirschi, 1969: 20).

Attachment to school, then, refers to the feelings an individual has about a school or the degree to which a youth cares about his or her school. In this instance, feelings may refer to an individual's sense of belonging, feelings of pride in the institution, and perception of safety while in the institution.

Another dimension of attachment, when discussing school bonding, is attachment to school personnel and particularly classroom teachers (Maddox & Prinz, 2003; Cernkovich & Giordano, 1992).[2] This facet of attachment includes interpersonal bonds forged between youth and their teachers. These connections are reflected in the student's reverence, concern, and esteem for the school staff (Cernkovich & Giordano, 1992).[3] Attachment to educators also can include a perception of being understood and supported by school personnel.

This attachment to the school and school personnel controls individual behavior. Hirschi (1969) argued that fondness for the school and or personnel will reduce participation in antisocial or delinquent behavior, and lead to more prosocial beliefs and attitudes such as respect for school property and personnel, a sense of community within the school and among students, and an overall perception of school safety. Dornbusch and colleagues (2001) support Hirschi's conceptualization that school attachment can act as a protective factor against the initiation into delinquency, but note school attachment does not adequately predict the intensity of this delinquency after onset.

School Commitment

Commitment addresses the extent to which individuals are invested in conventionality or have a "stake in conformity" (Akers, 1997: 87). School commitment is conveyed by the priority the school holds for the student, as well as the student's investment in school activities. Students who are highly committed to the school accept the goals, norms, and values of the school (Crosnoe, Erickson, & Dornbusch, 2002; Simons-Morton, et. al., 1999; Free, 1994; Cernkovich & Giordano, 1992; McGee, 1992; Hirschi, 1969; Polk & Halferty, 1966). The mechanism that drives an individual's conformity is the desire to adhere to the ascribed rules to maintain the value of the school and school related activities. Highly committed students do not wish to jeopardize what they have or could have by engaging in delinquency or other antisocial behaviors.

For example a student from a low income area may have a strong desire to attend college. The only way he or she could afford to pay for the college degree is through a scholarship, so this student would not want to risk using drugs or being involved in delinquency for fear that his or her chances at an academic or athletic scholarship may be threatened. When a student has high levels of academic or athletic aspiration, that student should be less likely to engage in antisocial behavior so as not to jeopardize his or her future plans.

School Involvement

Involvement refers to an individual's participation in conventional activities as they are related to school. In many instances measures of school involvement are operationalized in terms of frequency of attendance at school events such as sporting events (Maddox and Prinz, 2003). Another measure of school involvement is the number of hours a student spends in extracurricular activities such as yearbook, band, or other school-sponsored clubs. Hirschi (1969) would argue that spending time in more conventional settings, such as in school-based activities, limits the desire and amount of free time a student has to engage in delinquent activities.

When students are spending their time under adult supervision, as in the case of involvement in school activities, they have less time to engage in delinquent behaviors. These conventional activities, and the adult supervision that is present in school-based activities, preclude time for delinquency. When students are involved in school activities they spend more pro-social time with their peers under the supervision of the faculty advisors or coaches, increasing the level of school bonding.

While Hirschi (1969) contends that there are four distinct elements to the social bond, Cernkovich and Giordano (1992) contend that school involvement is actually a component of school attachment, suggesting that involvement is a demonstration of a student's fondness for the school. There is a strong correlation between an individual's fondness for the school and willingness to participate in activities. School attachment refers to the emotional connection to the social institution, whereas school involvement is a behavioral measure which demonstrates ties to the institution.

Belief in School

Belief is the acceptance of the values and norms of the school. When an individual endorses the rules of society as legitimate and valid, he or she is less likely to act in a delinquent manner. Belief in school is the most difficult component of the bond to develop, primarily because of the low levels of empirical support for this dimension in the study of school bonding (Williams, 1994; Cernkovich & Giordano, 1992).

The differential measurement is one of the largest problems in empirically testing the belief component of the school bond. There is little consensus across studies as to the operationalization of belief. While most studies have measured the component of belief as the norms and values of society, Patricia Jenkins (1993) defined belief as the norms and values specific to the school environment. Jenkins conceptualized belief specific to a student's perception of fair and consistent enforcement of school rules. Jenkins was one of the first researchers to define belief in terms of the students' perception of enforcement within the school. With this operationalization of belief, Jenkins (1993) found a significant relationship between students' belief in the fairness and legitimacy of school rules and school delinquency. This again lends support to Hirschi's (1969) social control theory.

Belief may also be conceptualized as a conviction towards school, or the idea that there is a value placed on education. As school involvement was a behavioral representation of attachment to school, belief may reflect school commitment. Students belief that they will go to college or achieve good grades is closely linked to the number of hours they study a night or amount of homework they complete, in other words commitment to school. In fact, one may argue a feedback loop develops between an individual's beliefs and level of commitment to school. Beliefs are translated into behaviors, representing a commitment to school, which feeds back to reinforce the beliefs.

Structural Theories and School Bonds

While Hirschi's control theory has been substantiated by research in explaining the control of individual level behavior, there are additional factors that need to be fleshed out when considering the school environment.[4] As Robert Merton explained in his theory of anomie, there are social structures in place that exert pressure on the individual to engage in "conforming" behaviors (Merton, 1938). Merton emphasizes that to explain social behavior we need not simply view the individual behavior, but must understand the context to which this behavior is taking place.

Cohen (1955) furthered Merton's reconceptualization of anomie, suggesting that holding all individuals to a particular set of norms and values can produce a form of strain. Cohen's work is particularly relevant when studying social institutions such as the family or education. In his work studying delinquent boys, Cohen (1955) made note of how social institutions such as schools present a very different experience for individuals from different socioeconomic backgrounds.

A number of American public schools uphold the middle class value system, which produces a strain on individual students who do not meet the expectations of such a value structure.[5] This institutional strain results in status frustration for some students who cannot meet the "middle class measuring rod" of the school. This suggests that a student's socioeconomic background could play a role in his or her success in the school. Specifically the student who comes from a middle class background will experience less strain and therefore adapt more easily to school than the student from a lower class background without the middle class value structure. Some research questions the relationship between social class and delinquency when controlling for school context (Kelly & Balch, 1971; Reiss & Rhodes, 1963).

Walter Miller (1958) suggested that lower socioeconomic status individuals do not necessarily experience status frustration; rather their behavior is a result of the values and norms embodied in their lower-class culture. Miller argues that "focal concerns" such as toughness, excitement, and trouble are characteristics of the lower class culture which, in turn, place children from these environments at a higher risk for delinquency than those from the middle or upper class cultures. Both Miller and Cohen acknowledge a mismatch between the middle class value system present in schools and the value system brought to the school by lower class youth. Cohen addresses similar issues in the comportment standards as well as academic preparedness as a difference found in the "college boys" as opposed to the "street corner" boys

Integration of Individual- and Structural- Level Theories
An argument can be made for the inclusion of the school environment in the study of bonding. For individuals to be at a lower risk for delinquent activity, they must have attachment, involvement, commitment, and belief in a social institution that provides a pro-social or a normative value structure. The education system is set up to provide these norms and values to the students, however, the environment may not necessarily fit each individual student.

In order for students to be involved, the school environment must provide them with avenues for involvement. However, with the current budgetary crisis in many states, the way to alleviate some of the fiscal burden is to cut extra-curricular activities. In addition, to believe in the norms and values of the society, the norms and values taught in the school should reflect those that are present in the home and in the everyday life of the child. As strain theories suggest, this is not always the case in public schools. It is possible for the student to experience a culture conflict within the school environment leading to possible status frustration.

This culture conflict and/or status frustration could also lead to a disjunction between the school's expectation of commitment and the individual commitment to school. For many students coming from low-income families the opportunity for college or advanced degrees may not be as quickly assumed as those from more privileged families. In addition, the familial expectations do not necessarily include college for the child. The culture of some families is to value a more vocational education so that the student could add financially to the family. Higher education is not always a priority. This causes a discord between what is expected from the family and what is expected in the school. Again, the dissonance between the individual commitment to school and the school's expectation is a further source of strain on the individual.

In addition, in order for an individual to endorse the rules and norms of a given environment, these policies must be perceived to be in the best interest of the students, the use of discipline in the school being one example. If a student feels as if he or she is an undeserving target of discipline by a teacher and/or the school, it becomes more difficult for him or her to develop a pro-social bond within that environment. Thus, if these policies are not perceived to be in the best interest of a particular group, it would be difficult for that group to endorse these rules as legitimate and valid.

Nevertheless, the student-school bond should act as a protective factor against delinquent or antisocial behaviors. The school bond, as with other social bonds, should insulate individuals from negative behaviors by providing a mechanism of social control which helps to reinforce appropriate norms and values as well as manage behavior. Given that both students and schools do not exist in a vacuum, the mechanisms that facilitate the individual development of a student-school bond, *both at the individual and school level*, should be identified in order to assist with school and social interventions leading to a reduction in delinquent behavior among the school aged population.

As previously discussed, there has been little research on school bonding that has *simultaneously* accounted for the individual level behaviors as well as the context of the schools. While Jenkins (1995) attempted to incorporate both individual and school level effects, her study of a single school could not address the effect of school context on the individual's bond with the school as an institution. This research attempts to build on the works of Cernkovich and Giordano (1992) and Jenkins by employing Hirschi's social control theory to explore the individual-level predictors of the student-school bond, then extending the theoretical concepts of social control to include school-level predictors of school bonding.

Review of the Literature

As mentioned in the introduction, students spend a large portion of their young lives in school. After the family, school assumes the responsibility of teaching a basic curriculum as well as educating youth on the appropriate behavior that is expected in society. School-based socialization, like socialization in the home, is intended to educate and empower youth on how to become responsible, productive adults. As children grow and develop, school-based activities and exercises in socialization become more formalized.

Preschools and early elementary programs, which in many cases are a child's first experience with structured learning, focus on group learning which is often separated by skill level (Lee, 2000). In addition to spending time in group settings, young children also spend most of their time in one classroom, with a single teacher who instructs them and their peers.[6] While this is changing as elementary schools more frequently employ ability grouping for reading and mathematics, the context is still at the most nurturing point of their academic career. In elementary school, children usually receive a lot of external guidance and direction from both parents and teachers. Teachers usually monitor schoolwork and parents monitor homework carefully to make sure the child is comprehending assignments. This educational context changes as children mature.

As children grow into adolescents, they continue to experience education in the classroom setting, however now, they are transitioning from classroom to classroom and teacher to teacher all day. As children mature from elementary to middle school, students are exposed to different teachers in different classrooms, as well as a more diverse pool of classmates. A student is no longer stuck with one peer group, nor is this same peer group present in each of their classes. In many cases, the middle school environment is a melding of numerous elementary schools, thus students are experiencing new peers as well as a new school environment. Adolescents are faced with more choices than ever before, and have multiple opportunities to become involved in school activities. These children are also expected to exhibit a higher level of personal responsibility and self-motivation than in elementary school (Rudolph, et. al., 2001).

Implicit in this middle school environment is the idea that students who develop positive social bonds to their school will do well academically, as well as abstain from delinquent behavior (Lee, 2000; Simons-Morton, et. al., 1999). While students begin to get involved in activities such as sports and music in elementary school, this involvement grows during middle school and becomes more solidified in the high school environment.

As students grow both socially and intellectually, they begin the process of self-selection into peer groups, extracurricular activities, and even academic or vocational expertise. Schools respond to these needs by staffing high school classrooms with teachers specialized in particular subject matter. Thus, as students pass from middle school into high school, they are again faced with new peers, new teachers, and in many cases a number of new classrooms specialized to serve their academic needs (Lee, 2000). Most high schools have a classroom for each subject, thus students could see up to 6 or 7 teachers a day. This is a dramatic shift from their experiences in the nurturing elementary school environment.

It is important to note that within the school environment students are engaging in formalized as well as informal learning (Lee, 2000; Simons-Morton, Crump, Haynie, & Saylor, 1999). While they may learn academic material from their teachers, their peer group is also having a dramatic influence on behavior. As students move from the nurturing environment of elementary school to the more specialized environments of middle and high schools, they are sharing social experiences with other youth who may have otherwise remained unknown to them. It is during these interactions that students can have their informal education in delinquency. In addition, with the growing amount of freedom and reduction in the amount of direct surveillance by teachers as one passes from elementary to middle into high school, students are able to find ways to bend, break, or in some cases shatter the rules.

The transition from elementary to middle school is very difficult for most children. As students, these children are confronted with new demands associated with the differences in classroom structure, school environment, academic standards, and teacher expectations (Rudolph, Lambert, Clark, & Kurlakowsky, 2001; Eccles, 1998; Eccles &

Midgles, 1989). These transitions bring a lack of consistency, changes in the academic environment, and an increase in ambiguity regarding the criteria for evaluation and success. Students struggle to successfully maneuver their way through the new environment.

The changes experienced during this transition year place students at high risk for negative or delinquent behavior during the first or crisis year. Research has found that the transition into middle school exerts adverse influences on adolescents such as lower levels of achievement, a reduced interest in school, negative attitudes towards learning, a disengagement from teachers and the classroom, and an increase in delinquency and drug use (Skinner, Zimmer-Gembeck, & Connell, 1998; Seidman, Allen, Aber, Mitchel, & Feinman, 1994; Wigfield, Eccles, MacIver, Reuman, & Midgley, 1991; Eccles, Midgley, & Adler, 1984). Though there have been modifications in the middle school environment to ease this transition period, many adolescents still feel overwhelmed by the changes (i. e. larger, more crowded schools, changes in the daily routine, higher expectations by teachers, and an increased emphasis on grades and future plans) (Rudolph, et. al., 2001). Students who are not equipped to or who believe they can not handle these changes tend to disengage from school and increase participation in delinquent activities, hence exhibiting a weakened school bond.

The problem of delinquency in schools is very complex. Who is responsible for delinquent acts when they occur in school? Does responsibility rest with the students, the parents, the teachers, or the schools themselves? Previous research is inconclusive on this topic. Some studies suggest that to predict violence and delinquency in schools, it is necessary to focus on the characteristics of individual students (Sprauge & Walker, 2000; Sugai, Sprauge, Horner, & Walker, 2000; Tobin, & Sugai, 1999). Other researchers suggest that the school environment should be the primary focus, suggesting that creating a pro-social school environment will reduce the level of delinquency in the schools (Nettles, Mucherah, & Jone's, 2000; Howard, Flora, & Griffin, 1999; Simons-Morton, et. al., 1999).[7]

Research suggests providing a young person with an environment that promotes trust rather than discord between the teacher and student will increase the student's social bond to school while reducing the chance of delinquency (Howard, Flora, & Griffin, 1999). Specifically, when students feel comfortable communicating with their teachers and administration, there is less friction between those in power (faculty and administration) and those who are perceived to be powerless (students) (Howard, Flora, & Griffin, 1999). If teachers and principals are disciplining the students in a way that is perceived to be unfair or have labeled a child as delinquent, students will exhibit negative affect towards or withdraw from the school environment resulting in weakened ties to the school (Kelly, 2001). Students who have a weak social bond to the school may feel that they have no other way to avoid conflict with other students, so they can resort to delinquency as a means of settling their disputes.

There are individual level factors that play a role in the individual's social bond to school. Attachment, commitment, involvement, and belief in school can be affected by a number of additional factors. A student's social bond to school can be affected by their background characteristics, familial involvement with their school, the individual's use of medicine to increase concentration, participation in delinquent activities, association with delinquent peers, and perception of school climate. While it is important to study the school environment in assessing the student-school bond, first individual differences must be taken into account.

Race

Previous research has indicated that individual demographic characteristics, such as race and gender can influence one's social bond to school. Research suggests that there is a qualitative difference in the school experience for African American students. Cernkovich and Giordano suggest a number of "empirical realities" that indicate racial differences in the school experience (1992:262). African Americans and Hispanics have a higher drop-out rate compared to adolescents (National Center for Education Statistics, 2003; DeParle, 1991).[8] There are charges of racially biased testing, negative attitudes towards minority students by teachers and lower teacher expectations for minority students than for white students (Davis & Jordan, 1994; Ogbu, 1988; Feldman & Saletsky, 1986). African Americans are also disproportionately disciplined in public schools (U. S. Department of Education Office of Civil Rights, 2001; England, Meier, & Fraga, 1988; Taylor & Foster, 1986) There is also evidence that the strongest predictors of achievement by whites, including family structure and parental involvement, are not as influential in predicting achievement of African Americans (Burke & Hoelter, 1988; Prom-Jackson, Johnson, & Wallace, 1987; Porter, 1974).

Educational achievement for African Americans comes about in a different way than for whites. Liska and Reed (1985) suggest that some African Americans view the institution of education itself as a false promise of equality, while others view it as the means to achieve the skills needed to compete on the free market. While education may be valued by some, there are still cultural road blocks that stand in the way of African Americans' social bond to school. The reality of discrimination in the workforce creates cynicism in the African American community in regards to the pursuit of higher education (Ogbu, 1988). While Cernkovich and Giordano (1992) found that there was no significance difference in the relationship between social bonds and delinquency between African Americans and whites, there is still evidence that race and ethnicity may differentially predict a student's social bond to school.

Jenkins (1993) found that middle school students perceive differential treatment of whites and non-whites particularly in the enforcement of the school rules. Qualitative interviews articulate how students perceive the racial bias among teachers in how they punish students. This inconsistent enforcement of the rules and recognition of teachers' racial bias towards students can lead to further disruption in the classroom as a result of unfair disciplinary practices. Jenkins (1993) would argue racial bias in the enforcement of school rules undermines a student's respect for the disciplinary process within the school; specifically minority students perceive themselves as targets of the larger school system. It is therefore hypothesized that being African American will reduce an individual's school bond.

Gender

The differences between boys and girls can be seen as early as infancy. At a very early age, girls develop a stronger level of self-control manifested in their ability to control emotions. As children begin the socialization process, girls are taught to maintain relationships, while boys are taught to value their freedom and independence. Girls, then, are dependent upon their relationships while boys run the risk of experiencing feelings of alienation. In the home, girls tend to be more supervised than boys, and are more likely to be controlled by their parents (Hagan, 1989). Parents or guardians may reward boy's risk-taking behavior, while punishing girls for similar behavior (Farrington, 1992).

Studies have consistently found girls engage in lower levels of delinquency than boys (Heimer & Matesueda, 1994; Elliot, Huizinga, Ageton, 1985; Canter, 1982; Hindlang, 1973). In addition, association with delinquent peers has been shown to significantly increase delinquency in males more so than females (Erikson, et. al., 2000). Since boys are more likely to engage in delinquent behaviors such as violence and drug use (see: Bachman & Peralta, 2002; Hickman & Piquero, 2001; Mazerolle, et. al., 2000), it is expected that being male will affect the school bond particularly when these behaviors occur within the school environment (Pestello, 1989).

One possible explanation for the higher rate of male delinquency in schools can be explained by their adaptation to social control mechanisms that are in place in the social environment (Hagan, 1989; Cohen, 1961). As children enter school, girls are more likely to be accustomed to the restrictive norms of the public arena. Therefore, girls are more amenable to the level of supervision found in the school, and are able to successfully act and react to their social environment (Thorne, 1993; Gilligan, 1991). As the school takes over the socialization of the children, girls continue to forge and value relationships while boys fight for their independence. Girls are more likely to develop attachments to teachers and other students in the classroom while also behaving in the traditionally appropriate manner or 'do school' (Gilligan, 1991). When girls 'do school', they remain invisible to adults and can negotiate school successfully, this is what differentiates the female school experience from the male school experience.

Boys have a more difficult time negotiating school. Boys mature more slowly and are more active than girls. These developmental differences, and the potential medical labels that come with these differences, may also attribute to the gender differences in school bonding. The fact that boys mature more gradually than girls means that girls will achieve cognitive milestone's earlier than boys, leaving the possibility for males to be misdiagnosed as learning disabled in the early grades. In addition, boys are far more active than girls, particularly in the early ages. Research indicates that boys are two to four times more likely to be diagnosed with attention deficit hyperactivity disorder (ADHD) than girls (Acia & Connors, 1998). The medicalization of misbehavior in boys has a significant effect on their self-concept and in many instances leaves the young boy feeling like a loser or failure. This negative self-concept does not lend itself to the development of prosocial bonds to school, particularly if it is school that reinforces the negative self-concept.

Further, studies have found boys to have difficulty identifying with their teachers as role models, particularly in the early grades (Sadker & Sadker, 2003; Cohen, 1955). In part this is due to the predominance of female teachers in elementary school and a lack of male role models. Studies have indicated that boys are far more successful in school when they have male teachers (Maccoby, 1998). In short, if girls have an easier time adapting to the behavioral constraints placed on them in the school setting, it is probable that girls will experience less social strain and thus are more likely than boys to develop a social bond to school.

In a study looking at programs in place to reduce violence and delinquency in schools, Eggert and colleagues (1994) found that behavioral interventions lead to a significant reduction in girls' association with delinquent peers while increasing school bonding. While they also noted an increase in the level of school bonding for boys, the male levels of delinquent peer associations remained strong regardless of behavioral interventions (Eggert et. al., 1994). This was an interesting result given Cernkovich and Giordano (1992) found that the effect of school bonding on delinquency was not as strong for females as it was for males.[9]

Based on this literature, it seems as if gender moderates the dimensions of the school bond. Cernkovich and Giordano (1992) found attachment, commitment, and belief to be most significant elements of school bonding for females, while involvement is most significant for males.[10] Nevertheless, gender plays a role in a student's bond to school. In short, it is hypothesized that males will experience lower levels of school bonding than females.

Further, it is expected that the model predicting the bond for males will differ from the model for females. If boys mature at a slower rate than girls, the older boys in a classroom may be more likely to experience a prosocial bond to school than younger boys.

Age

As previously mentioned, transitioning into the school environment can be a difficult thing for children and adolescents. As children mature and age, they begin to form salient social bonds such as those with their school or peers. In the school environment, most students are roughly the same age, and progress through educational endeavors together. Being older than one's peers, however, has been found to inhibit the development of prosocial bonds as well as to school leading to an increased risk of school drop out (McNeal, 1995; Elliott & Voss, 1974; Cervantes, 1965). Further, Bonny and colleagues (2000) found students who were older than the average "grade appropriate" age experienced higher levels of alienation and disconnectedness within the school. Feelings of alienation and disconnectedness would indicate a weak bond to school. Thus, it is expected that older students within a grade will experience lower levels of school bonding.

Family Structure
A study by Gove and Crutchfield (1982) suggests that family structure affects levels of delinquency in youth. Delinquency also reduces an individual's prosocial bonds including those to the family and school. When a child lives with one parent or a biological parent and a stepparent, research suggest the child's prosocial bonds are weakened and he or she is more likely to engage in delinquency (Chilton & Markle, 1972; Gove & Crutchfield, 1982). Burgess (1979) suggests that single mothers have less contact with their children, spending less time monitoring and disciplining their behavior. Aston and McLanahan (1991) support Burgess' findings with evidence that single-parent families indicate low-levels of parental involvement with school and social activities. If a student can get away with delinquency in the home, it is likely he or she would not understand why it is unacceptable in school. Further, when delinquency is not corrected in the home, but is in the school, a student may feel unnecessarily targeted by school discipline and disengage from education.

Travis Hirschi (1969) found that children who reside with a non-biological father are more likely to be delinquent than children living with intact families. When children come from intact homes, their parents are more likely to take an interest in their lives. Stepparents may not be as interested and involved with stepchildren and their school and social activities as biological parents. When stepparents do not monitor school activities or academic achievement, the children can feel ignored and lose respect for these adults. These feelings of neglect and lack of respect for stepparents may be generalized to other adult authority figures, such as teachers and school administrators (Hirschi, 1969). Children who lack attachments with their stepparents may not be concerned about the negative stigma that may be attributed to their parents/guardians if they get in trouble (Nye, 1973). Parents who are involved with their children, however, have a positive effect on their children's school behavior and academic achievement (Fehrmann, Keith, & Reimers, 1987).

Rankin and Wells (1991), however, challenge these ideas suggesting that family structure has an indirect effect on delinquency. In families where the child is in the custody of a single-mother, broad support systems may often develop to meet the familial needs. Relatives, neighbors, and other friends serve as support systems to the mother and positive agents of socialization for the children. This is particularly true in African American families (Billingsley, 1968; Taylor, Chatters, & Mays, 1988; Wilson, 1996, Edin & Lind, 1997). Research also suggests that, in some cases, the absence of a biological parent can actually improve the life of a child. Joan McCord (1983) contends that domestic tranquility in the home is more important than the presence of both parents in predicting delinquency. Children who come from homes exemplified by conflict are at greater risk of delinquency than children from broken, but peaceful homes (Nye, 1973; Emery, 1982).

Though research is inconclusive on the link between family structure and school bonding, enough research supports the correlation to suggest there is an effect. Thus, it is predicted that children who reside with a single parent or a parent and a stepparent are less socially bonded to school.

Parent's Level of Education

Research has indicated that student behavior is a function of parent's social standing, often operationalized in social research as educational achievement (Jenkins, 1995; Eckert, 1989; Cohen, 1955). Students, within the school setting, may be predisposed to certain social groups based on the socioeconomic standing provided by their parents (i. e. , "Brains"—middle to upper class students who conform to the expectations of the school, "Losers"—lower or working class youth who reject the school norms and value structure). Social science research indicates parent's educational attainment may influence a student's delinquency as well as the level of school bonding (Jenkins, 1995; Meyers, et. al. 1987; West, 1982). Parents with higher levels of education are more likely to encourage their children to be more productive and involved in school, and may be more effective and comfortable interacting with teachers and school administrators than less educated parents. West (1982) suggests that parents who have achieved a higher level of education are more likely to provide educational resources in the home, including assisting with homework. Further, parents with higher levels of education expect a higher level of educational achievement from their children, as well as encourage future educational aspirations (i. e. college, graduate/professional school) (Paulson, 1994; Steinberg, 1993; Myers, Milne, Baker, and Ginsburg, 1987; Cohen, 1955). Parents with higher levels of education are likely to discuss the benefits of post-secondary or higher education and encourage children to be more productive in their academic endeavors. Thus, it is expected that parent's educational achievement will have a positive effect on a student's bond to school.

Grade Point Average

Academic performance is an important factor to consider given its predictive relation with future life outcomes. Research indicates there is a relationship between school bonding and academic performance, as measured by grade point average (GPA). Academic performance is enhanced when students exhibits stronger bonds to school (Maddox and Prinz, 2003; Lopez, Ehly, & Garcia-Vazquez, 2002; Learner & Kruger, 1997; Wiatrowski, et. al., 1982). Those students who exhibit higher grade point averages are found to report a stronger bond to school. While this relationship between academic achievement and the school bond it correlational, it can be argued that grade point average predicts a student's commitment to school. Academically successful students were found to be more likely to be committed to and involved in school where as lower GPA students were found to reject the goals and values of education (Metz, 1979). Thus, it is expected that students with higher grade point averages will exhibit a stronger bond to school.

Delinquent Peers

As children develop, parents are the primary means of socialization. Between the ages of 8 and 14, however, children begin to seek the approval of friends and peer associations. Friends begin to have a greater impact on the lives of children, and soon supercede the influence of both parents and school (Berndt, 1986). Thus, as peers become more salient in the lives of children, their social bonds to peers become stronger and the norms and values of these peers will be increasingly important.

Hirschi argues that attachment to peers is important in controlling delinquency; he indicates that the most important thing in deterring delinquency is that an individual is attached to "others" (Akers, 1997).

But what if the attachment is to delinquent peers? Hirschi contends that "...the more one respects or admires one's friends, the less likely one is to commit delinquent acts" (Hirschi, 1969: 152). However, research contradicts this position. Researchers have consistently found that association with delinquent peers is a strong predictor of individual delinquency (Warr & Stafford, 1991; Matsueda & Heimer, 1987; Tittle, Burke, & Jackson, 1986; Elliot, Ageton, & Canter, 1985; Akers, Khron, Lanza-Kaduce, & Radosevich, 1979). Delinquency is a group activity. Harris (1998) suggests that peers are able to influence juveniles in a way that no parent or other authority figure can.

The desire to conform to peers' norms, values, and standards is more important to many youths than the nurturing norms and values of their parents. Juveniles spend approximately 6 hours a day with their peers in the school environment, during which they are able to foster a bond with their peers. It is during adolescence that individuals value membership as part of a peer group. One's peer group usually consists of school friends who share similar interests and beliefs. In many cases, these kids become friends because they are in the same classes or are in the same academic track. As students distance themselves from their parents and foster a strong bond with their peers, social standing is increasingly important. These students begin to engage in face work to manage their identity within the only environment where they perceive they can exert their independence--school. Thus, juveniles are committed to being members of their cliques or crowds and do not want to lose their social status, particularly in a school setting.

Peer associations can have an effect on a student's school bond. Specifically, if a student were to associate with a non-delinquent group who all place a strong emphasis on academic achievement, this student would likely also hold academic achievement in high regard and maintain a solid bond to school. If a student associates with a delinquent peer group, however, it is likely that values of that peer group would be counter to those of the school, and as such a reduction in the student-school bond would be expected.

Substance Use

Maddox and Prinz (2003) suggest that substance use may decrease an individual's school bonding. Following Hirschi's (1969) control theory, prosocial bonds would delay onset into delinquent behaviors such as substance use, as well as reduce current levels of participation (Eggert & Kumpfer, 1997; Hawkins, et. al., 1997; Catalano, et. al.,

1996). Murguia and colleagues (1998) found that a student's perceived acceptance by his or her teacher was negatively correlated with current drug use, association with drug using peers, and prior drug involvement. This can be interpreted to suggest that higher levels of attachment to school are correlated with lower levels of substance use. Eggert and colleagues (1994) found that behavioral interventions, such as intensive school based programming, not only reduced individual drug use, but also increased the school bonding among the experimental group.

A higher level of school bonding was found to be positively associated with lower levels of involvement in substance use (Byrant, Schulenberg, Bachman, O'Malley, & Johnston, 2000; Pilgram, Abbey, Hendrickson, & Lorenz 1998; O'Donnell, 1995). Many of these studies employed large national data sets, such as Monitoring the Future, allowing for nationwide generalization of substance use among youth.

Since most of this research has been correlational, there is no real directional causality suggested by the research. If an association between two variables is noted, it is feasible that the relationship could be in either direction. It is logical for causality to go both ways. Research suggests that students who use substances such as alcohol or illicit drugs are the one's who feel isolated from the school culture. When these students become involved in using drugs and alcohol, however, the effects of these substances are likely to further distance the student from school creating a mutually reinforcing disengagement from school. That is when a student is recovering from a hangover or currently experiencing the effects of a substance, he or she is not motivated or engaged in the learning process further aggravating the weakened school bond. This study will argue that higher levels of substance use will reduce the levels of school bonding.

Delinquency
There is considerable empirical evidence that supports the association between weakened school bonds and individual delinquency (Simons-Morton, et. al., 1999; Wade & Brannigan, 1998; Zhang & Messner, 1996; Free, 1994; Jenkins, 1995; Cernkovich & Giordano, 1992; Freidman & Rosenbaum, 1988; Liska & Reed, 1985; Hirschi, 1969), substance use (Simons-Morton, et. al., 1999; Hawkins, et. al., 1997; Eggert, et. al., 1994; Free, 1994; McGee, 1992), and school dropout (Keith, 1999; Cernkovich & Giordano, 1992).

The student-school bond has also been examined to study patterns of bonding across race and gender groups. Cernkovich and Giordano (1992) looked at the impact of school bonding on African American and white students. This research found empirical support for control theory, concluding that the effects of school bonding on delinquency did not differ across race-sex subgroups.

Jenkins (1995) also deconstructed the student-school bond to predict school delinquency of middle school students. In addition to lending empirical support to the finding delinquency is significantly associated with weak student-school bonds, Jenkins' research identified commitment to school and belief in the school rules as the strongest predictors of delinquency in school. Another interesting empirical finding was that school involvement was the weakest of the four elements of the school bond (Jenkins, 1993).

Previous research has been successful at denoting a link between the school bond and delinquency. However, school bonding has mostly been used as a predictor of delinquent behavior. The decomposition of the four components of the school bond by Jenkins (1995) and Cernkoich and Gioradano (1992) suggest that certain mechanisms of the school bond have a differential impact on individual delinquency based on race and gender. Previous research, however, has not focused on the mechanism that creates the school bond in students.

While research is able to support one direction of causality, specifically that delinquency reduces the school bond; it may also be possible for this relationship between delinquency and school boding to be mutually influential. If low levels of school bonds are associated with higher levels of delinquency, it is feasible that the causality works in both directions. A weak bond to school may increases participation in delinquency; however, participation in delinquent behaviors could also result in a further reduction in the school bond. Thus the association between school bonds and delinquency are mutually influential. This research will assess what predicts a student's bond to school, testing the supposition that higher rates of delinquency will reduce the student's school bond.[11] Thus, it is expected that participation in delinquency will reduce a student's bond to school.

Importance of Including the School Environment

Students are at times more aware of the school environment than the teachers and administration. They know which kid is the class bully and which is the teacher's pet. Kids are also attuned to how they and others are treated by the faculty. Howard Becker (1952) observed that students are differentially treated, noting that teachers focused more attention on white middle-class students. Other research found that there was blatant discrimination and racism in the public school classroom (Kozol, 1967; 1991). This perception, however near or far from the truth, can become a reality in the mind of a child. Students who believe that the teacher is their friend, who are treated fairly, and participate in school activities, will theoretically have a stronger social bond with teachers and school as a whole. However, if they perceive that there is differential treatment by the faculty and administration, their social bond to school will weaken.

The school context impacts students choice of peers, availability of curriculum, and future aspirations. While these may differ between schools, it is important to understand the school context to assess the impact of the within school differences as well as between school difference. Studies suggest that while between-school differences have an effect on student success, it is the within-school processes which have a greater impact at the secondary school level (Alwin & Otto, 1977). Little research has addressed these issues at the elementary and middle school levels.

Proportion of Poverty within a School

In order for an institution to maintain social order, there must be a consensus on the norms and values that are shared by the individual members. When this consensus is reached, individuals feel more integrated and bonded to each other and the establishment.

The social institution of education socializes its members by using the norms and values held by the predominant middle class. While this may be a normative environment for the majority of students in public schools, there is still a group of students for whom these values induce delinquency. As previously mentioned, Albert Cohen (1955) found that public schools impose middle class expectations on students which produce strain within lower and working class individuals. Students who are unable to achieve status and acceptance by conventional middle class means are faced with status frustration[12].

Status in American society is achieved by conforming to norms of dress, behavior, and scholastic achievement (Akers, 1997). In public schools, individuals are confronted by these middle class norms by teachers, administration, and other students. Students who come from this middle class background may be more apt to conform to these rules of behavior and norms of appearance, while lower class students struggle with these standards (Cohen, 1955).

Those lower class students who do not exist under the same middle class value structure in the home may not have the same academic and social skills to meet the middle class standards (Cohen, 1955). For instance students from lower class families or those whose parents do not place a high value on education, may perceive that school will not benefit them in the future because there is a gap between their curriculum and their experience in the real world (Polk & Schaefer, 1977; Stinchcombe, 1978). The educational institution fosters such perceptions by the use of ability grouping, the superlative position of college preparatory curriculum, and the second-class ranking of vocational and technical programs in the school's curriculum (Lee, 2000; Gamoran, 1992).

The strain that is produced by the inability of these students to achieve academic success leads them to engage in delinquency which is in direct opposition to the middle class value structure (Cohen, 1955; Miller, 1958; Cloward & Ohlin, 1961). The inability to achieve social status or recognition by their peers may leave students feeling alienated in the school environment or with feelings of failure which lead to a weakening of the school bond or even the decision to drop out of school (Elliot & Voss, 1977; Thornberry, Moore, & Christenson, 1985). Public schools must be prepared to handle the issues that result from a class conflict that occurs when lower and working class students are immersed into a middle-class value structure.

Schools which have a high proportion of students in poverty may face barriers to effectively educating all students. Students who come from poverty or lower class families may act out in disruptive or violent ways just to garner some enjoyment from the school experience (Czikszentmihalyi & Larson, 1978). These disruptions may not only affect the students but also create a level of frustration among their teachers that may in turn lead to a reduction in the ability of students to foster a social bond with the school.[13] Schools with frustrated teachers, disengaged students, and high rates of school disruption will experience a lower mean level of school bonding among their students.

In short, the school can have an impact on the individual's behavior. American public schools impose a middle class value system on all students regardless of their background. The institution, however, neglects to account for the diversity of the population. Specifically, schools fail to acknowledge that students come from different economic backgrounds with differing goals for this education process. The middle class value that is placed on college preparatory curriculum and the institutional stigma that is placed on technical or vocational programs foster feelings of alienation and help to induce delinquent behavior by reducing the ability of all students to develop a strong social bond to the school. So, schools that have a high proportion of students in poverty will have lower mean levels of school bonding experienced by their students.

School Size
Research indicates that school climate is related to delinquency in schools (Cernkovich & Giordano, 1992). Some studies examine school size as a factor in student behavior. Toby (1993) found that smaller schools, with more individualized attention by the teacher, have fewer disruptive incidences. Byrk and colleagues (1993) assert that small school settings operate more like a community rather than a bureaucracy. This finding reinforces the idea that smaller schools foster more of a bond among faculty and students. When there is a disruption in class, the teacher may be able to handle the situation in the classroom rather than referring it out to the principal. In many larger schools, however, teachers and students do not have a personal relationship and in many cases do not feel safe, and as such the attention is diverted from instruction to individual safety (Ascher, 1994). When there is a disruption in class, the teachers are less likely to attend to the problem themselves for fear that their personal safety and the safety of the other students may be compromised. Instead, they remove the problem from the classroom which results in an official sanction by the principal. Thus, larger schools will experience a lower mean level of bonding among students compared to smaller schools.

Ability Grouping in Schools
Another factor the affects the school climate is ability grouping. Ability grouping, formerly called tracking, is an educational technique that groups students based on their scores on intelligence tests and level of academic achievement. This is a tool that is omnipresent in the U.S.

public school system (Epple, Newlon, & Romano, 2002; Gamoran, 1992). Reese and colleagues (1996) reported that less than 15 percent of eighth graders and less than 11 percent of tenth graders were in classrooms that did not group students by ability level; however, the high schools and middle schools do not readily acknowledge this much ability grouping in the school. The use of ability grouping is also pervasive at the elementary school level (Oakes, et. al., 1992).

Ability grouping has been shown to impact students' academic achievement and level of delinquency (Gamoran, 1992; Wiatrowski, et. al., 1982; Kelly, 1978; Kelly, 1976; Kelly, 1975; Shaefer, Olexa, & Polk, 1972). As with the perception of the school environment, children are astutely aware of their classification and what status (or stigma) that classification carries. Students who are placed in non-college grouping are more likely to drop out, not participate in extracurricular activities, and are disproportionately disciplined compared to students in the college bound groups (Shaefer, Olexa, & Polk, 1972). These findings suggest that students in lower tracked classes are less attached to and involved in school than their college bound counterparts. And whether it is differential treatment by teachers, or simply a higher level of delinquency among these individuals, ability grouping has an effect on the level of delinquency in a school (Wiatrowski, et. al., 1982). Thus, schools that employ ability grouping will have lower mean levels of school bonding experienced by their students.

The Effect of Delinquent Schools on School Bonding
Research has shown that students with school discipline problems are at higher risk for dropping out of school and for involvement in juvenile delinquency (Altenbaugh, Engel, & Martin, 1995; Gottfriedson & Gottfriedson, 1985). Recently, teachers report that violence and disruption are increasing in the classroom and negatively impacting the school climate (Tobin & Sugai, 1999).

Between six and nine percent of juveniles are responsible for more than half of the serious disciplinary referrals (i. e. weapons violations, fighting) in elementary and middle schools (Horner & Walker, 2000; Skiba, Peterson, & Williams, 1997). Note that this is a small percentage of the school population that is engaging in serious delinquency. Early discipline problems in schools have been linked to delinquency in the community as well as maladjustments in adulthood (Loeber & Farrington, 1998; Walker, Colvin, & Ramsey, 1995).

Since 1993, students between the ages of 12 and 18 have been more likely to be victims of certain "in-school" crimes such as threats or physical injury (School Crime and Safety; 2000, 2001)[14]. Children are also engaging in more acts of delinquency such as physical fights on the school property (School Crime and Safety, 2001). For example, in 1999, middle and high school students were victims of approximately 880,000 crimes while attending school (Indicators of School Crime and Safety, 2001)[15]. These incidents of victimization include having something stolen, being engaged in a physical fight, and having possessions vandalized.

A closer look at school climate indicates certain behaviors, such as fighting and bullying, detract from the learning environment. Schools with a high prevalence of fighting or bullying may instead foster an environment of fear and intimidation (School Crime and Safety, 2001). During the first six months of the 2000 academic school year, September 2000 to January 2001, approximately 14 percent of students participated in a physical fight and five percent reported being bullied in the past six months (School Crime and Safety, 2001). When a student is the victim of bullying or other victimization, it is likely that he or she may be distracted from academic work. When there is a high level of delinquency present in the school environment, the level of school bonding at that school will be reduced because students will be less likely to be attached and committed to school.

School Disciplinary Response to Misbehavior and Delinquency

Confronted by the fear of violent behavior in schools, educators are being asked to make schools safer and figure a way to discipline the small percentage of students who engage in serious delinquency. However, schools receive little guidance or assistance in their attempt to establish and sustain pro-active disciplinary systems. Research suggests that existing discipline information could be utilized to identify problem students within each school, though it is not a fool-proof method of reducing discipline problems (Mulvey & Cauffman, 2001).

Sugai and colleagues (2000) suggest that discipline referrals may be better employed as an indicator of the status of school-wide discipline and their response to delinquency in school. They propose discipline referrals may also improve the precision with which schools enact discipline to address the most severe behavioral problems. Consequently, the discipline measures of a school will provide an indication of behavior management school-wide, predicting how rule enforcement influences a student's bond to school.

When a student becomes disruptive in the classroom or on school grounds, he or she is usually reprimanded and sent to the principal. This often results in a discipline referral that is recorded by the administrative staff. Discipline referrals do not solely measure poor behavior among students. They also measure the level of observation by teachers and staff, as well as the commitment of the school administrative staff to document each occurrence in writing (Sugai, et. al., 2000). Consequently, discipline referrals are not simply a measure of individual behavior, but also a measure of discipline within the school environment (Sugai, et. al., 2000).

There are many ways a school can discipline delinquent behavior. Students can be placed in detention, suspended, or expelled. Detention is handed out for minor violations, and there is little if any standard for issuing this punishment. A student can receive a detention for not handing in a homework assignment, talking back to the teacher, or even engaging in mild forms of delinquency such as smoking in the bathroom. When a student engages in a more serious behavior, or adds up enough minor behaviors that warranted detentions, the student is suspended from school for a period of time, usually one to three days where he or she must attend school, but is away from the other students. In many cases, the 'in-school suspension' is held under the supervision of the school principal. Finally, the most severe punishment is expulsion. Expulsion is the removal of the student from the school for a set number of days.

The new trend in response to violence and threats of violence is the implementation of zero-tolerance policies. Zero-tolerance policies set rules for the behavior of all students in the school with a predetermined expulsion for violation of the appropriate rules. Critics argue that zero-tolerance policies do not foster perceptions of safety in schools as intended. Instead, they evoke fear and anti-social behaviors in the students (Mulvey, & Cauffman, 2001). Rather than form a bond with the teachers and administrators, students feel alienated and perceive an adversarial relationship with school officials. Moreover, research has found that students are withholding information from the administration to avoid disproportionate punishments (Mulvey & Cauffman, 2001)[16].

Resnick and colleagues (1997) propose that students who feel they are being treated fairly by the school administration and other students are less likely to engage in delinquent behaviors. This suggests that when punishment is exacted in a fair manner, it can decrease the level of delinquency and increase the bond to school. However, more often when punishment is disproportionate in the school, it can reduce the bond to school by breeding distrust of teachers and school administrators among students who feel targeted.

Suspension as Primary Means of School Discipline
Schools, in response to the increase in school delinquency, violence and disruption, have tightened their security measures and discipline policies (Tobin & Sugai, 1999; Rutherford & Nelson, 1995). Schools that once ignored idle threats are now reacting with increased discipline. A school's discipline climate results from an interaction between the demographic characteristics of students and faculty and the organization of the school (Arum, 2000; Devine, 1996). In many cases, the teacher makes the decision to discipline a student. For instance, a teacher who cannot manage a student's behavior will send him to the principal.

Suspension is one of the most common responses to behavior problems in elementary and secondary schools (Tobin & Sugai, 1999; Ketterlinus, Lamb, & Nitz, 1994). Schools believe that removing the "dangerous" or "disruptive" students from the premises, regardless of their physical or emotional condition is necessary in order to maintain a safe and orderly school environment (Tobin & Sugai, 1999). Removing the potential disruption and/or threat from the classroom would provide a more academic environment, and in turn promote a stronger bond to school among the remaining students. These instances however are rare and research indicates that school discipline actually leads to alienation and a further reduction in the student-school bond.

Altenbaugh et. al. (1995) and Bowdich (1993) argue that suspension interrupts a student's education; repeated school sanctions (i. e. suspensions, expulsions) can lead to alienation or eventual school dropout. Some students may feel that they are not free to exert their new-found independence. Other students who perceive that the school is targeting them, or feel alienated from potential involvement in school activities would be hypothesized to have a reduced level of school bond. Thus, it is expected that schools that report handing out a high proportion of discipline referrals will experience lower mean levels of school bonding.

Social Development, the School Context, and the School Bond

There are a number of factors that play into the student-school bond relationship. It is clear that while previous research has focused on the individual level factors that impact the school bond-delinquency relationship, some have even accounted for the school environment. However, few if any have attempted to study the student-school bond across the three major transitions of schooling.

While Hirschi's (1969) control theory does not directly address issues of social development among youth in school, it is a topic that requires attention for this analysis. Catalano and Hawkins (1996) reconceptualized the school bond by integrating a social development model that provides a framework from preschool to adolescence. Like Hirschi (1969) the social development model posits a prosocial attachment (or bond) to others deters an individual from delinquent behavior. In addition to the concept of deterrence, the social development model proposes three factors essential for establishing a social bond. The first is opportunities for involvement, or occasion for students to interact with one another through school related activities. Second, skills for involvement, are social skills that allow students to establish and foster interpersonal relationships. Last is reinforcement of involvement, or some sort of incentive to participate or maintain involvement in a particular social activity (Catalano & Hawkins, 1996; O'Donnell, Hawkins, & Abbot, 1995; Hawkins et. al., 1992).

The social development model posits that involvement is a precursor to the social bond, not a component of the bond as Hirschi (1969) proposed. Involvement is conceived as a mechanism for establishing a social bond, which must be available to the student else a bond may never form. Throughout an individual's development, opportunities for involvement must be made available by the schools to enable individuals to cultivate a school bond. The need for schools to provide opportunities for involvement continues to reinforce the importance of the school environment in the study of school bonds.

Elementary school students have many opportunities to interact with their peers during the school day, such as lunch or recess; however, there is little to no opportunity for extracurricular activity. During this stage of development education is very structured and formalized. Peer-to-peer interactions are closely monitored and in many cases facilitated by parents rather than by school. This is the time in a child's life where the parents and family are the primary agents of socialization. When these children get involved in activities, such as dance class or organized sports, it is usually with the assistance of their parents. During this time, children develop the skills necessary for interaction in other social arenas (Catalano & Hawkins, 1996).

Participation in community activities, however, is qualitatively different from participation in school-based activities. Community activities, in many cases chosen by the parent, do not always involve students with a diverse group of their peers as would be found in school-based activities. Parents have more control over the peer group with which their child interacts by choosing the activities in which the child participates. Community based activities can be costly, and only children whose parents can afford the activity are able to participate. For instance, football can be an expensive activity for children. Community "pee wee" football leagues require the child to purchase their own equipment as well as their own travel to and from games.

As children progress on to elementary school, family remains an important agent of socialization but school also plays an important role in teaching the necessary skills for interaction with peers. These skills are necessary for the transition from elementary school to middle school. It is during middle school when the child experiences the most diverse influences; including family, school, and peer group (Catalano & Hawkins, 1996). While parents may be hopeful that their prosocial influence will lead their children to prosocial peers, this is not always the case.

The middle school environment is ripe with social transitions, providing many prosocial and antisocial opportunities for involvement (Lee, 2000; Simons-Morton, et. al., 1999). It is during this turbulent time when bonds to family are weakened in favor of stronger bonds to peers, in part because parents are less welcome in middle and high schools. Again, due to the change in social setting, an adolescent has a wide variety of opportunities available to him/her that may have otherwise gone unknown were it not for the school environment. Adolescents are able to join clubs, participate in sports, be a part of a band, and also interact with other peers; the avenues for involvement in middle school are open to the student. Catalano and Hawkins (1996) suggest that parents and family lay a solid prosocial framework in early childhood and continue to nurture these bonds through adolescence, since the bonds to peers and school remain important throughout high school (also see Maddox & Prinz, 2003).

High school is a period when peers and society exert the strongest influence (Maddox & Prinz, 2003). Further, high school is a time where the student experiences the most independence. With this independence comes a greater opportunity for involvement. This independence also leads to increased exposure to and interaction with both prosocial and antisocial peers and adults, again increasing the risk of participation in delinquency (Maddox & Prinz, 2003; Lee, 2000). Many high school students, by the time they reach the 11th grade, have part time jobs that provide them with disposable income. These part time jobs create social bonds outside of the school, and in some cases are not always prosocial.

Bachman and colleagues (2003) found that students who choose to work at earlier ages tend to be more disengaged from school. In addition, during high school, school disengagement by means of part time employment is also highly correlated with substance use and other delinquent behaviors among students. In addition, Safron, Schulenberg, and Bachman (2001) found that work intensity, or more hours worked, was closely linked to a reduction in students participation in school activities, sports, and other healthy behaviors and an increase in students participation in substance use or delinquent activities. In other words, high school students who work more hours in a job are more likely to engage in substance use and other delinquent behaviors.

The social development model suggests there are significant differences between the elementary, middle, and high school experience. It is expected that the variation in the school environment will become increasingly important in explaining the school bond. Specifically it is expected that the between school differences will be greatest among the high school population and least among the elementary school population.

Overview of this Research
Sociological research has focused on a student's bond to school as a protective factor against delinquency. While this is one important component in the study of delinquency, it is also important to understand what impacts the school bond. Specifically, what creates a strong student-school bond among elementary and secondary school students and how does it change during the transition from elementary to middle and into high school?

Employing Hirschi's (1969) theory of social control, this study will model the social bond to school while accounting for both individual- and school-level stimuli. Specifically, this study will look at the effect of individual-level characteristics such as race, gender, educational attainment of one's parents, reports of delinquent activities, and association with delinquent peers on the social bond to school. In addition, this study will incorporate school-level factors, such as minority enrollment, school poverty, use of ability grouping, and the use of discipline in the school, to simultaneously model direct and moderating effects (between school-level and individual-level factors) on the overall student-school bond.

This project will include both individual and multi-level analyses to assess the impact of demographic and family characteristics, participation in delinquent activities, association with delinquent peers, as well as characteristics of the school attended on students' bond to school.

The following chapter will present the specific research hypotheses and methodology for this project. Chapter 2 will present hypotheses for the individual-level predictors on the school bond as well as school-level predictors on the mean social bond found within a school. The methodology addresses the data collection for the individual and school-level data, the variables used for this analysis, and the statistical techniques employed for this study.

Chapter 2:
Research Hypotheses and Methodology

Research Hypotheses

The review of the literature on the topic of school bonding has aided in the development of research hypotheses. These hypotheses have been shaped by previous research findings as well as limitations to previous studies. Given the scope of this project, there are a number of expectations derived from the existing literature as well as a set of research hypotheses for both the individual- and school-level analyses.

At the individual level, the school bond is measured as an individual student's attachment, commitment, and involvement in school. Thus, at the individual level, the models are predicting an individual's social bond to school. Existing literature indicates that the model predicting school bonds will vary by race and gender (see Cernkovich & Giordano, 1992). Thus, while it is not directly stated as a research hypothesis, it is expected that the model of school bonding will not be equivalent across the genders, nor across racial and ethnic categories. That is, the process of developing a school bond is different for males versus females, as well as different across racial and ethnic categories. As such, this expectation will be confirmed by utilizing the Chow test (see: Chow, 1962) to determine if the model of bonding is equivalent across racial and ethnic groups. In addition, a set of individual-level hypotheses will be directly tested in this research. They are as follows:

H1: Being African American will reduce an individual's bond to school.

H2: Being male will reduce an individual's bond to school.

H3: Older students within a class will experience less of a bond to school than those who are at or below the mean age of a class.

H4: Students who live with both their parent will have a stronger bond to school.

H5: High average levels of parents educational attainment will increase an individual's bond to school.
H6: As individual grade point average increases, so will one's bond to school.
H7: Association with delinquent peers reduces an individual's bond to school.
H8: Individual drug use reduces one's bond to school.
H9: Participation in delinquent activities will reduce the bond to school.

This research, while addressing variables that predict an individual's bond to school, will also address the impact that school level variables have on individual outcomes. In addition to the individual level outcomes, a shift will be made to look at the school environment and the impact it has on the average bond within that school. It must be made clear, then, that there will be a shift in the interpretation of the measure of school bonding. While at the individual level school bonding was the measure of an individual's attachment, commitment and involvement in a school, at the school level, school bonding becomes a measure of the average level of school bonding found in a given school. In short, the individual measure of school bonding shifts to an average measure of school bonding when accounting for school level characteristics.

The body of literature that exists on schools and the school environment also indicates a set of consistent findings that provide a set of expectations for future research in the field. The school experience is as unique as the individual. Though there may not be a vast level of diversity across schools, there is still the expectation that the level of school bonding will vary across the schools in the sample. At the same time, it is expected that a significant amount of the variation in school bonding can be explained by school-level variables such as school size, use of ability grouping, level of poverty, and overall delinquency levels found in the school.

In addition, there are a number of developmental differences found between elementary, middle, and high school environments. Utilizing the operationalization of social bonds as identified by Hirschi (1969), it is expected that the average level of school bonding will increase as students mature from elementary to middle to high school due primarily to the increased opportunity for involvement in the school, the developmental move away from family and towards peer groups, and the autonomy of those who do not wish to be in school to drop out when in the 10th grade.[17] Existing literature assisted in the development of the following research hypotheses:

H10: The higher the proportion of low-income students in a school, the lower the mean level of school bonding within a given school.
H11: Larger schools will experience lower average levels of school bonding.
H12: The use of ability grouping in a school decreases the mean level of bonding in that school.
H13: School bonding will be lower in high delinquency schools.
H14: Those schools with high numbers of suspensions and expulsions assigned as punishment will experience lower average levels of school bonding in the school.

Students do not exist independently of their school environment, and as such there is an expectation that there will be moderation effects between individual- and school-level variables. The following hypotheses indicate how the individual-level effects can be moderated by school-level variables. These hypothesized interactions are as follows:

H15: Schools with an above average level of delinquency will decrease the average level of school bonding for a male within that school, widening the already significant gender gap.
H16: In schools with an above average proportion of minorities enrolled, African American and Non-African American minority students within that school will experience a higher average level of bonding.
H17: Schools that report an above average level of punishment imposed upon students will have a negative impact on African American and Non-African American minority students, increasing the minority effect.
H18: The negative impact of delinquency on school bonding will be greater in those schools which employ ability grouping than in those which do not.

The following section will describe the methods employed to test the aforementioned hypotheses.

Methods
The following section describes the method of data collection, sample characteristics, variables employed in the analysis, and statistical analyses utilized to test the research hypotheses. Since this analysis will employ both individual-level and school-level data, it may be helpful to describe the layout of the remainder of the chapter.

The methods section begins with a brief description of the 'state' survey utilized to gather data from 5th, 8th, and 11th grade students and how those data were collected. Next the individual-level survey is described, followed by a description of the individual-level variables that will be used in the analysis. This section continues with a description of the school-level instrument, data collection, and variables employed in this analysis. Finally, the chapter concludes with an explanation of the statistical analysis techniques and brief summary of the chapter.

The State School Survey
The State School Survey is a confidential and anonymous questionnaire that has been administered annually to most 5th, 8th, and 11th grade classrooms since 1989. This survey is conducted through the Center for Drug and Alcohol studies at a major Mid-Atlantic University, and is part of that state's State Incentive Grant Cooperation Agreement from the Substance Abuse and Mental Health Services Administration's Center for Substance Abuse Prevention.

The state school survey is used to collect data regarding the experiences of students in elementary and secondary public schools in the state. Each year, research staff take this survey into 5th, 8th, and 11th grade classrooms throughout the state. The surveys are handed out in an anonymous classroom administration, by University personnel rather than by teachers or school administrators. This is done to increase the students' perceptions that their individual results will not be seen by school personnel. Each grade is administered a survey written in an age appropriate manner.[18]

Data Collection
The 2000 school survey was administered between the months of March and June. At least one week prior to the administration, a parental consent form was sent home with students. With Internal Review Board approval, the parental letters were written in a manner of passive consent. The parents only returned a signed slip if they wished

their children not to participate. Once the parents were notified of the administration, the surveys were taken into the school. The students with parental consent were asked to voluntarily complete the survey. They were also free to discontinue filling out the survey or to skip any questions they did not choose to answer at anytime during survey administration.

Surveys were completed in all 16 public school districts in the state. After data collection was complete, those surveys where students reported using fictitious drugs or otherwise falsified their answers were excluded from the sample and subsequent analysis.[19]

The 5th grade questionnaire requested demographic information on the students, their academic achievement, and how they spend their time. The survey also included questions regarding their perception of the school environment, other students, and safety in the school and in their neighborhood. The remainder of the questionnaire asked the students about their and their peers' experiences with alcohol and drugs, as well as their perceptions of alcohol and drug use.

The 8th and 11th grade questionnaires covered the same content areas as the 5th grade, as well as included questions regarding the students and their peers' participation in delinquent activities, such as carrying a weapon to school, trespassing, fighting, and truancy. There is also information regarding participation in school activities, feelings of depression, and propensity towards risky behaviors (i.e. going to wild parties, participating in illegal activities, and doing things that are scary).

Student Sample Characteristics
The sample consists of individual level self-report information on 5,503 5th graders, 5,136 8th graders, and 3,901 11th graders across 114 schools. This accounted for 67 percent of the state's 5th grade enrollment, 60 percent of the state's 8th grade enrollment and over 50 percent of the 11th grade enrollment. The data were compared on demographic characteristics to the total public school enrollment in this state. These results are displayed in Table 2.1.

Table 2.1: Comparison of Survey Respondents to Public School
Enrollment in the State

	5th Grade		8th Grade		11th Grade	
	Sample	State	Sample	State	Sample	State
African American (% of sample)	1484 (26%)	2625 (31%)	1232 (34%)	2757 (30%)	837 (22%)	2018 (27%)
White (% of sample)	3556 (62%)	5212 (61%)	3564 (61%)	5752 (63%)	2643 (68%)	5025 (67%)
Non-African American Minority (% of sample)	463 (8%)	678 (7%)	340 (7%)	631 (7%)	421 (11%)	506 (7%)
Sample Total (% of grade enrollment)	5503 (66%)	8515 (100%)	5136 (56%)	9140 (100%)	3937 (52%)	7549 (100%)

The racial/ethnic breakdown of students in each sample was also found to be similar to the statewide racial and ethnic distribution (see table above). Each sample was found to adequately represent the race/ethnic distribution for school age students in the state. The 5th and 11th grade sample underrepresent African Americans by roughly 5 percent as compared to the state enrollments. The 8th grade sample; however overrepresents African Americans. The statewide 8th grade population represents 30 percent of all 8th grade students, whereas African Americans comprise 34 percent of the 8th grade sample. The 5th and 8th grade sample mirrors the Non-African American and White enrollments in the state. Finally, while the 11th grade sample equally represents the White 11th grade population in the state, there is an overrepresentation of Non-African minorities in the 11th grade sample as opposed to the state enrollment. Though there was variation across the sampling distribution, it can be argued that each sample provided enough variation to be representative of the population found in each grade level, allowing for reliable estimates across race and ethnicity.

In addition, the 5th, 8th, and 11th grade samples were each composed of approximately 49 percent males and 51 percent females. This is again representative of the approximate 50/50 gender split found in the 5th, 8th, and 11th grade classrooms across the state during the 1999-2000 academic year, and can provide reliable estimates by gender (see: http://www.doe.state.de.us).

Variables in the analysis

Independent Variables
Variables such as *sex, age, and race of student* are taken directly from the survey. *Sex* is the student's self-classification as either male or female.[20] The *sex* variable is scored 1 for "male" and 0 for "female". The *age* measure asks the students how old they are to which they are able to respond in age appropriate choices.[21]

Students were asked to describe themselves as "White", "Black", "Native American(Indian)", Mexican or Chicano", "Puerto Rican/ Other Latin American", "Oriental/Asian", "White and Black", or "Other".[22] Due to the lack of variation in the sample, the *race* variable was broken down into three dichotomized variables. The first variable identifies an individual as *African American*. It was scored 1 for "African American" and 0 for any other racial category. Those individuals identifying themselves as Native American, Mexican or Chicano, Puerto Rican/Other Latin American, Oriental/Asian, or Other were combined into a variable measuring *non-African American minority*. This variable was scored 1 for "Non-African American minority" and 0 for white and African American. The final race variable "White" was scored 1 for "White" and 0 for all other racial categories. In the case of this analysis, the dummy variables for African American and Non-African American Minority will be placed in the model for analysis, leaving "White" as the comparison group.

The question for academic achievement or *grade point average* asks the students to "describe [their] grades this year" as mostly "A's", "B's", "C's", or "D's or F's". This variable was then transformed so that there was a numerical *grade point average* associated with the letter grade category. The *grade point average* variable has a range of 1.0 to 4.0 where 1.0 represents "mostly D's or F's", 2.0 represents "mostly C's", 3.0 represents "mostly B's", and 4.0 represents "mostly A's".

The *living with both parents* question asks "which of the following [that the student] live[s] with most of the time", "two parents", "one parent and one stepparent", "mother only", "father only", "grandparents", "other family member", "non-family member".[23] Again, due to a lack of variation across all possible responses, this variable was further dichotomized to measure "living in with both parents" versus "not living with both parents". A student coming from an intact two-parent family was scored as 1 and a student coming from any another family structure, including a parent plus a step-parent, was scored as 0.

A proxy measure for individual level socioeconomic status was derived utilizing a *parental education* measure for the 8th and 11th grade students. No such proxy was available for the 5th grade population. The survey asked 2 questions "what was the highest level of education your mother/ female guardian completed" and "what was the highest level of education your father/male guardian completed". Each of these variables was coded in the following fashion: 1 'completed grade school or less', 2 'completed some high school', 3 'completed high school', 4 'completed some college', 5 'completed college', 6 'graduate or professional school after college', 7 'don't know'. For purposes of this analysis, this variable was recoded to increase the range of the possible scores mimicking a truncated continuous variable. Each response was recoded from its original code into the corresponding number of years in school.[24] The 'don't know' categories were coded as missing.

The *parental education* variable was created accounting for the family structure present in the respondent's home. If the respondent resided with both parents, a parent and a step-parent, or 2 guardians, the *parental education* variable was created by averaging the sum of the maternal education score and the paternal education score. If the respondent only lived with one parent, the *parental education* variable was the score of that parent (mother or father) with whom the child resides.

The *individual delinquency* measure was different for the 5th grade than for the 8th and 11th grade. For the 5th grade only, a univariate measure of *fighting* was used as the *individual delinquency* measure. The survey asked the student "have you been in a fight at school this year'. The variable was coded "yes" or "no", and dichotomized so that "yes" was the category of interest.

The variable that measures *individual delinquency* for the 8th and 11th grade is computed as a scale. The scale is additive so that the higher the score on the scale, the higher the level of individual delinquency (possible range of 0.0 to 32.0). This scale is composed of variables that measure how often the student would "take a weapon to school", "take part in a fight", "go into a house/building when [they] are not supposed to be there", "steal something from a store", cheat on a test in class", "sneak money from an adult's wallet/purse/other place", or "gamble for money or possessions". Each of these variables ranged from 1 to 5 where 1 represented "never", 2 represented "before but not in the past year" 3 represents "a few times in past year", 4 represents "once or twice a month", and 5 represents "once or twice a week". The *delinquency* scales for both grades were considered to be reliable with reported alphas of 0.82 for the 8th and 0.78 for the 11th grade.

The *drug use* variable was again an additive scale (possible range 0.0 to 48.0) measuring the frequency of drug, alcohol, and tobacco use among 5th, 8th, and 11th grade respondents. In the 5th grade, drug use measures frequency of use of the following: cigarettes, cigars, chewing tobacco, alcohol, marijuana, downers, uppers, inhalants, hallucinogens, crack, powder cocaine, and over-the-counter drugs to get high ($\alpha=0.72$). The student was asked how often they used each of the aforementioned drugs, with potential answers ranging from "never" to "almost every day". Each of the variables ranged from 1 to 6 where 1 represented "never", 2 represented "before but not in the past year" 3 represents "a few times in past year", 4 represents "once or twice a month", and 5 represents "once or twice a week", and 6 represents "almost every day".

The 8th ($\alpha = 0.85$) and 11th ($\alpha = 0.82$) grade *drug use* variables are a bit more complex. These drug scales asked for a self reported frequency of use of the following: cigarettes, cigars, clove cigarettes, downers, uppers, inhalants, hallucinogens, crack, power cocaine, designer drugs (such as ecstasy), PCP, heroin, and over-the-counter drugs to get high. Again, the student was asked how often they used each of the aforementioned drugs, with potential answers ranging from "never" to "almost every day". Each of the variables ranged from 1 to 6 where 1 indicated "never", 2 indicated "before but not in the past year" 3 indicated "a few times in past year", 4 indicated "once or twice a month", and 5 indicated "once or twice a week", and 6 indicated "almost every day".

In addition to these drugs, two additional variables were included to measure frequency of alcohol and marijuana use over the past year. To determine frequency of alcohol use, the student was asked "how many times have you had a drink of alcohol, beer, wine, liquor, mixed drink in the past year". The variable was then coded from 1 to 6 where 1 represented "0 times", 2 represented "1-2 times", 3 represented "3-5 times", 4 represented "6-9 times", 5 represented "10-19 times", and 6 represented "20 or more times". Marijuana use was measured in the same fashion. The student was asked "how many times have you smoked marijuana (grass, pot, hash, weed) in the past year". Again the variable ranged from 1 to 6 with the same coding as the alcohol variable. Like the 5th grade, both the 8th and 11th grade drug scales were additive so the higher the score on the scale the more frequent the individual drug use.

The final individual level independent variable measures *delinquent peers*. The reliability measures for this variable are as follows: 5th grade α = 0.67; 8th grade α = 0.89; and 11th grade α = 0.87. The questions in the scale ask the student to report on their friends' behavior. This is a scale that combines reports of how many of the respondent's friends smoke cigarettes, get drunk at least once a week, smoke marijuana, skip school at least once a month, have been stopped by the police, shoplift, and have damaged or destroyed property that does not belong to them.[25] In the 8th and 11th grade questionnaires, each of the aforementioned variables range from 1 to 5, with potential responses ranging from "none", "a few", "some", "most", or "all". Each of these responses was coded in ascending order, so that in an additive scale, a high score represents a student with a more delinquent peer group (possible range 0.0 to 36.0).

Dependent Variable: School Bond
The scale used to measure the *social bond to school* in the 8th and 11th grade is comprised of measures from three of the four components of Hirschi's (1969) social bond; attachment to school and school personnel, commitment to school, and school involvement.[26] The surveys did not contain a measure of belief with enough face validity to include in this analysis.[27] The score on the *social bond to school* scale represents the level of the student-school bond. The reliability for these scales is within an acceptable range. The alpha for the 8th grade school bond variable was 0.68 and the alpha for the 11th grade was 0.73.

These values are within an acceptable range of reliablity for the field of sociology (Agresti & Findlay, 1999).

The *attachment* component of the bond is comprised of two measures representing an individual's attachment to teachers or school. The first measure of attachment to personnel is represented by the question asking how often the student "gets along with teachers at school". The second measure of *attachment* measures a sense of belonging within the school as measured by how well the student "gets along well with other kids at school". The responses for each of these variables ranged from 1 to 5, representing "most of the time", "often", "some of the time", "not often", "never". The variables were then reverse coded so that "never" was coded as 1 and "most of the time was coded" as 5.

The second component of the school bond, *commitment to school,* is measured by four variables. The first is "the amount of time spent studying or doing homework outside of school". This measure of time spent doing homework was coded from 1 to 5 where 1 represents "none", 2 represents "less than an hour", 3 represents "one to two hours", 4 represents "two to four hours", and 5 represents four or more hours". The next two measures of school commitment ask how often the students talk to [their] parents/guardian about how school is going, and talk to [their] parent/guardian about career plans. Both of these variables are measured from 1 to 5 where 1 represents "never", 2 represents "before but not in the past year", 3 represents "a few times in past year", 4 represents "once or twice a month", and 5 represents "once or twice a week". Finally, the last component of the *social bond* scale measuring school commitment asks "how much schooling do you think you will complete". Again, codes range from 1 to 5 with 1 representing "probably will not finish high school", 2 representing "complete high school degree", 3 representing "some college", 4 representing "complete college degree", and 5 representing "graduate or professional school after college".[28]

Finally, involvement in school was measured by three separate variables; is the student "involved in extracurricular activities", "a member of any school athletic team", and how often the student "attends events at school in the evenings or on weekends". The variables asking about membership in school-based activities were coded dichotomously where 1 represents "no" and 5 represents "yes".[29] The variable measuring the frequency with which a student attends school events was coded from 1 to 5 where 1 represents "never", 2 represents "before but not in past year", 3 represents "a few times in past year", 4 represents "once or twice a month" and 5 represents "once or twice a week".[30]

The *school bond* variable for the 5th grade respondents was quite different from the 8th and 11th grade measures. Due in part to the difference in reading comprehension as well as developmental differences, the 5th grade school survey did not include identical questions to the middle and high school questionnaire. The limitations of the survey only allowed for measures of attachment to school and commitment to school. There were no measures of school involvement or belief in pro-social norms within the school.

The score on the *social bond to school* scale represents the level of the student-school bond. The alpha reliability for the 5th grade scale was 0.46. This is a low level of reliability for the field of sociology; it would fall within the range of moderate reliability (Agresti & Findlay, 1999). This reliability estimate suggests that over half of the score can be attributable to error, which is more than is suggested by measurement theory (Carmines & Zeller, 1979). While it is not within a range of "good" reliability, it is not so low that it cannot be used for this analysis.

The *attachment* component of the 5th grade students' bond is comprised of three measures representing the child's attachment to teachers or school. The first measure of attachment to personnel is represented by the question asking how strongly the student agrees with the statement "I get along with teachers at school most of the time". The second and third measure of *attachment* evaluates a sense of belonging within the school as indicated by an positive response when asked if a student "likes school" and "feels safe in school". These variables were dichotomous, and coded so that 1 represented "yes" and 0 represented "no".

The second component of the school bond in the 5th grade, *commitment to school,* is measured by only one variable. This measure of school commitment asks if the student "talks to [his/her] parents/guardian about how things are at school". Again, this is a dichotomous measure which is coded so that 1 represents "yes" and 0 represents "no".

School-Level Variables

The Elementary and Secondary School Survey

The mission of the U. S. Department of Education, Office for Civil Rights (OCR) is *to ensure equal access to education and to promote educational excellence throughout the nation through vigorous enforcement of civil rights laws* (http://www.ed.gov/OCR). The OCR Elementary and Secondary School Survey (E&S Survey) is employed to gather data regarding the nation's public elementary and secondary schools (http://www.ed.gov/OCR). Specifically, the purpose of this data is to monitor the pervasiveness of inequality in the form of discrimination and civil rights violations and ensure that schools are in compliance with "Title II of the Americans with Disabilities Act of 1990" (http://www.ed.gov/OCR). In short, this data helps to monitor for any act of discrimination on the basis of race, color, national origin, sex, age, and disability in public education programs and activities that receive federal financial assistance (http://www.ed.gov/OCR).

Data Collection

As noted previously, the E&S Survey collects trend data regarding the nation's public elementary and secondary schools. Conducted since 1968, the E&S survey is a federally mandated survey sent to a random sample of the nation's school districts. Every two years the E&S Survey is sent to one-quarter of all public school districts. In 2000, OCR conducted a sample of all school districts to coincide with the 2000 U. S. Census. The 2000 E&S Survey contains information on 14,681 public school districts and 88,648 schools within those school districts. Of those 88,648 schools, 182 were in the same state as the student survey and can be utilized for this analysis.[31] The specific school-level data from this survey was requested from the State Department of Education to ensure the accuracy and validity of the records.

Information regarding the percentage of students that receive free and reduced lunch from the school was collected from each of the school districts. This information is public knowledge, and is posted on the 19 districts' websites. The percentage of students receiving this service was obtained directly from the State Department of Education and merged into the OCR school database, matching the new variable with the appropriate school in the current database on the federal school identification number.

School Sample Characteristics

School-level data were collected on 182 public, charter, alternative, and vocational schools throughout the state.   In order to match the individual- and school-level data, a number of schools and subsequent student data had to be removed from this analysis. Though all 182 schools in the state were represented in the school-level data (via the E&S survey), not all of these schools participated in the student-level school survey. Those schools that were not included in the student-level survey were removed from the analysis. In addition, the state school surveys provided student-level data on students from several private or parochial schools. The data from these students were also removed from the sample given that the E&S school survey was only conducted among state public schools.

After merging the individual self-report data with the school-level data from the Elementary and Secondary School Survey, 105 schools were included in the sample consisting of 43 elementary schools, 31 middle schools, and 31 high schools. The following table is provided to demonstrate the representative nature of the school level data.

Table 2.2: Comparison of Schools in Sample to the Population of Schools in the State [32]

	Elementary School w/ 5th grade	Middle School	High School	Districts
Sample	43	31	31	16
State Total	44	32	32	16
Percentage of Total	97%	97%	97%	100%

As demonstrated by Table 2.2, 97 percent of the elementary, middle and high schools across in the state are represented in this analysis.

School-Level Variables in the analysis

The variable measuring the *use of **ability grouping*** was taken directly from the E&S survey. The Department of Education, through the E &

S survey, asked schools if "they *ability grouped students in Reading or Mathematics?*" This was coded as a dichotomous variable (1="yes", 0="no"), so that "yes" was the reference category.

The total *enrollment* variable was also taken directly from the E & S Survey. The survey asked for the school principal to report the total number of students present in their school during the 1999-2000 academic year. This variable is a count of the number of students enrolled during school year.[33] The total enrollment number was then cross-referenced to the information provided by the state Department of Education for additional verification and to ensure the validity of the response.

While some school-level variables could be taken directly from the E&S survey, certain variables needed to be derived for this analysis. The variable for *minority enrollment* was calculated by summing the number of "African American", "American Indian", "Hispanic", and "Asian" students reportedly enrolled for each of the schools in the sample. This transformation provided a count of how many minority (or non-white) students were enrolled for each of the schools in the sample. The variable for *minority enrollment* was then transformed from counts into proportions, and multiplied by 100 to generate a percentage. For example, to calculate the percent of African American students in each school, the total number of African American students was divided by the total enrollment of the school and then multiplied by 100. The result is a percent of African American students enrolled in each school.

To measure the amount of *discipline in a school,* four variables: number of students disciplined using corporal punishment, suspensions, expulsions, and zero tolerance policies were summed together to create a count of the number of students per school that have been formally disciplined. To control for the differences in the size of the schools, this count of the number of students disciplined per school was further transformed into a proportion of students punished as a function of the total enrollment of the school. To do this, the total number of students disciplined per school was divided by the total enrollment in that school and then multiplied by 100 to create the rate of punishment in the school.[34]

The *proportion of low-income students* was derived using the information from the state Department of Education and the E&S survey. The state provided the number of students per school who received free and reduced lunch. In order to receive free and reduced lunch in the year 2000, the student's family must fall below 185 (reduced lunch) and 130 (free lunch) percent of the poverty level (National School Lunch Program, 2000). To calculate the proportion of students in poverty in each school, the number of students receiving free and reduced lunch was divided by the total school enrollment. This number was then multiplied by 100 to indicate the percentage of students in a school from low-income families. While this is not a perfect measure, it does provide some proxy as to the potential proportion of students who may experience social strain given that they fall below the middle class measuring rod.

The variables for *average level of delinquency per school* and *average drug use* were created using information from the school survey. Each individual student's delinquency and drug use score within the school was summed to provide an estimate of the total amount of delinquency per school. This total was then divided by the number of individual student respondents per school. So, for each school, the individual delinquency score for each student was summed and then divided by the number of respondents for that particular school. Therefore, the variable for *school delinquency* estimates the average level of delinquency of survey respondents in each school.

Statistical Analysis
This study employed a combination of Ordinary Least Squares Regression and Hierarchical Linear Modeling (HLM) to explore the veracity of each hypothesis.[35] In order to correct a problem with missing cases, the means of each variable were substituted for the missing values in the analysis.[36] The individual-level variables were run in an ordinary OLS regression model to get a sense of the amount of variation explained by the individual-level variables without the influence of the school variables. In other words, the OLS model presents the between-student results for each grade level.

The individual-level variables were then placed into a hierarchical linear model (HLM) in order to further test the estimation of individual effects on the mean level of school bonds as well as model the cross-level effects between the individual- and school-level on the school bond. The value of employing hierarchical linear modeling is that we are then able to look at these individual-level predictors within the context of the school-level measures.

Rationale for using HLM

Multilevel modeling, such as HLM, is actually a series of regressions. In fact HLM performs regressions on regressions. These regressions begin with the lowest level of analysis within the next highest unit of analysis, and are used to specify the effect of the social context on the outcomes at the individual-level (Byrk & Raudenbush, 2002). Sociologists have long argued that individuals respond to their social environment and researchers should, therefore, account for the context of the behavior as well as the behavior itself. Multilevel modeling, such as HLM, enables researchers to explore the individual-level effects on an outcome as well as accounting for the cross-level effects such as school context on individual behavior.

Despite the prevalence of hierarchical data structures in social science research, previous studies of school bonding have often failed to adequately address them in data analysis. This methodology enables researchers to account for organizational data structures in hierarchical linear modeling.

Hierarchical linear modeling (HLM) has many benefits over traditional methods; primarily it allows researchers to simultaneously model effects at different levels of the data (see Byrk and Raudenbush, 2002). First, it is beneficial to understand what Byrk and Raudenbush (2002) mean when they discuss the different levels of analysis. Organizational data is structured in a way where there are many possible levels of analysis, all of which could possibly have some effect on the others. So, to study school bonding among elementary and secondary school students, the fact that students are nested within schools must be accounted for, and there might be differences not only across students but also interactions with school level variables as well. Hierarchical linear modeling will allow for the simultaneous modeling of these potential effects.

While these are important advantages over other statistical methods, the key advantage of hierarchical linear models is their ability to model variation in an individual-level (level-1) model as a function of a school-level (level-2) model. Again, when studying school bonding, the key question becomes whether some of the difference in the level of school bonding across students can be explained by differences across schools. For example, the mean effect of being male on school bonding will be a function of school variables such as ability grouping and school size. Thus, individual variation is modeled as a function of differences across schools.

Model for Analysis

The first level of analysis is the basic OLS regression equation. This is to model the level-1, or individual-level predictors within a school. This equation is defined in the same fashion as the basic OLS regression equation:

Level-1:

$$Y_{ij} = \beta_{0j} + \beta_{1j}x_1 + \beta_{2j}x_2 + \beta_{3j}x_3 + \beta_{4j}x_4 + \beta_{5j}x_5 + \beta_{6j}x_6 + \beta_{7j}x_7 + \beta_{8j}x_8 + r_{ij}$$

In this equation, we can see that Y, or level of school bonding of a student in a given school j, is a linear function of nine independent variables ($x_1 \ldots x_9$); age (x_1), gender (x_2), race (x_3), parental education (x_4), living with both parents (x_5), GPA (x_6), individual delinquency (x_7), individual drug use (x_8), association with delinquent peers (x_9), and a residual term (r_{ij}).[37] The intercept (β_{0j}) can be interpreted as the expected level of school bonding of a student in the jth school, when all the independent variables equal zero. Each slope (β_{ij}) can be interpreted as the expected change in school bonding for a one-unit increase in the independent variable, holding all other independent variables constant in the jth school.[38] The error term (r_{ij}) represents the unique effect associated with the individual person in the jth school.

In order for the outcomes to be interpretable in this model, the continuous individual-level (level-1) variables were centered around the group mean. In order to center the variables around their group mean, the school mean for each variable was subtracted from their score such that the new mean would now equal 0. Since the dichotomous variables had a meaningful '0' value, defined as not the dummy category specified (i.e. female vs. male or white vs. black), they were left in their natural metric for this analysis.[39] The continuous variables, once centered around their group mean, can be interpreted based on the difference from the school mean. In other words, the value for individual delinquency can now range from a negative number to 0 to a positive number instead of from 0 and above (See Arnold, 1992).

To form the level-2 (or school-level) equations, the parameters (intercept and slopes) from the level-1 (individual-level) equation become the outcomes at level-2 and are influenced by school-level predictors. Therefore the intercept (β_{oj}) at level-1 becomes a linear function of W_j, or set of independent school-level variables and a residual term, υ_j. Each of the slopes $(\beta_{1j} . . . \beta_{8j})$ also becomes a linear function of the set of school-level independent variables (W_j). For example, being 'male' is a predictor of the student-school bond at level-1. The effect of being male, however, becomes an outcome influenced by a set of school-level variables (such as school size or ability group) in the level-2 analysis. The mean effect of being male on the school bond depends upon the school size or the use of ability grouping in a school.

For this analysis, the level-1 (individual-level) coefficients were modeled as randomly varying. This was accomplished in two ways depending on the level-1 (individual-level) variable. The level-2 (school-level) intercept (γ_{00}), the level-1 (individual-level) coefficient to randomly vary across level-2 (school-level) units, but in this case, there is an attempt to model the variation. An example equation for this model is $\beta_{oj} = \gamma_{00} + \gamma_{01} W_j + \upsilon_{0j}$, where γ_{00} is the expected mean level of school bonding when all level-1 (individual-level) predictors are held at 0, γ_{01} is the expected change in the mean level of school bonding given a unit increase in W_j, and υ_{0j} is the unique effect of school j on the mean change in the level of school bonding holding W_j constant. The level-1 (individual-level) predictors, were also allowed to randomly vary across level-2 (school-level) units, again with an attempt to explain the variation. This is seen in the equation: $\beta_{oj} = \gamma_{00} W + ... \upsilon_{0j}$. The research question focused on the how the variation at level-2 (school-level) af.fected the outcome, in addition to the cross-level variation between the level-1 (individual-level) and level-2 (school-level) variables.[40]

These level-2 (school-level) equations become:

$$\beta_{0j} = \gamma_{00} + \gamma_{01} W_1 + \gamma_{02} W_2 + \gamma_{03} W_3 + \gamma_{04} W_4 + \gamma_{05} W_5 + \upsilon_{0j}$$
$$\beta_{1j} = \gamma_{10} + \gamma_{11} W_1 + \gamma_{12} W_2 + \gamma_{13} W_3 + \gamma_{14} W_4 + \gamma_{15} W_5 + \upsilon_{1j}$$
$$\beta_{2j} = \gamma_{20} + \gamma_{21} W_1 + \gamma_{22} W_2 + \gamma_{23} W_3 + \gamma_{24} W_4 + \gamma_{25} W_5 + \upsilon_{2j}$$
$$\beta_{3j} = \gamma_{30} + \gamma_{31} W_1 + \gamma_{32} W_2 + \gamma_{33} W_3 + \gamma_{34} W_4 + \gamma_{35} W_5 + \upsilon_{3j}$$
$$\beta_{4j} = \gamma_{40} + \gamma_{41} W_1 + \gamma_{42} W_2 + \gamma_{43} W_3 + \gamma_{44} W_4 + \gamma_{45} W_5 + \upsilon_{4j}$$
$$\beta_{5j} = \gamma_{50} + \gamma_{51} W_1 + \gamma_{52} W_2 + \gamma_{53} W_3 + \gamma_{54} W_4 + \gamma_{55} W_5 + \upsilon_{5j}$$
$$\beta_{6j} = \gamma_{60} + \gamma_{61} W_1 + \gamma_{62} W_2 + \gamma_{63} W_3 + \gamma_{64} W_4 + \gamma_{65} W_5 + \upsilon_{6j}$$
$$\beta_{7j} = \gamma_{70} + \gamma_{71} W_1 + \gamma_{72} W_2 + \gamma_{73} W_3 + \gamma_{74} W_4 + \gamma_{75} W_5 + \upsilon_{7j}$$
$$\beta_{8j} = \gamma_{80} + \gamma_{81} W_1 + \gamma_{82} W_2 + \gamma_{83} W_3 + \gamma_{84} W_4 + \gamma_{85} W_5 + \upsilon_{8j}$$
$$\beta_{9j} = \gamma_{90} + \gamma_{91} W_1 + \gamma_{92} W_2 + \gamma_{93} W_3 + \gamma_{94} W_4 + \gamma_{95} W_5 + \upsilon_{9j}$$

Where β_{0j} ... β_{9j} are the mean level of the coefficients at level-1 (individual-level) on the school bond within a school and the W's represent the independent variables at level-2 (school-level). The independent variables at level-2 are as follows: school enrollment (W1), the use of ability grouping (W2), minority enrollment (W3), proportion of students disciplined (W4), and proportion of students on free and reduced lunch (W5).[41] The effect of each school-level predictor, without interaction with the level-1 coefficients, on the mean level of school bonding in a school is found in the β_{0j} equation. The other models (β_{1j} ...β_{9j}) represent the mean effect of each of the level-1 coefficients on the school bond as it depends on each of the school-level predictors. The decision was made not to center the level-2 (school-level) variables, leaving them in their natural metrics for this analysis. While the intercepts in the level-2 (school-level) models depend upon the location of the W_j variables, the estimates are not affected (Byrk & Raudenbush, 2002).[42]

To interpret the first equation, the mean level of school bonds when all other variables at both levels are held at zero is represented by γ_{00}, and γ_{01} represents an expected change in the mean level of school bonds with each additional student enrolled in a school. The effect of ability grouping on the mean level of school bonding is represented by γ_{02}, while γ_{03} indicates the expected change on the mean level of school bonding with each percent increase in the minority enrollment in a school. Finally, the expected change in the mean level of school bonding with each additional percent of the school population disciplined is represented by γ_{04}, and the expected change to the mean level of school bonding with a percent increase in the proportion of students receiving free and reduced lunch is symbolized by γ_{05}.

The additional level-2 (school-level) slopes $(\gamma_{1j}...\gamma_{9j})$ are interpreted as the average effect of the level-1 (individual-level) variable $(\beta_{1j} ... \beta_{9j})$ on school bonding. So in this instance, the equation for β_{1j} will predict the average effect of age on school bonding. The equation for β_{2j} will predict the average effect of being male on the level of school bonding. The equations for β_{7j} and β_{8j} will predict, respectively, the average effect of delinquency and drug use on the level of school bonding. In addition, the new coefficients $(\gamma_{j1}W_1 ... \gamma_{j5}W_5)$ can be interpreted as the mean effect of the respective school-level variable on the effect of the individual level variable. For instance $\gamma_{21}W_1$ can be interpreted as the mean effect of school enrollment on the average males' school bond, such that the effect of being male on school bonding depends upon the enrollment in a school.

Summary

Utilizing self-report data from 5,780 5th graders from 43 different elementary schools, 5,136 8th graders from 31 different middle schools and 3,901 11th graders across 31 different high schools, this study will model the student-school bond. In particular, this study will simultaneously account for individual and school level effects on the level of school bonding in an elementary, middle, and high school population.

The following chapters will present the results of the analysis. The results will be presented beginning with the elementary school sample in chapter 3, followed by the middle school sample in chapter 4, and finishing with the high school sample in chapter 6. Chapter 7 will conclude this study by offering a conclusion, policy recommendations, and ideas for future research on the topic.

Chapter 3
School Bonds in Elementary School

Fifth grade is a time of development and transition. Fifth grade children, usually between the ages of 9 and 11, maintain a strong bond to their parents; however their peers are beginning to play a more significant and salient role in their young lives. Given the primacy of the parent-child bond, it was hypothesized that the attachment to school is only in the fledgling stages of development. Students in the 5th grade will experience some school bonding, most of which is a reflection of the importance placed on education by parents in the home.

Compared to middle and high schools, the elementary school environment nurtures the student. While students are continuously gaining more freedom, they are still carefully monitored and cared for by school staff. Students remain reliant on their parents and their community for social activities, only beginning to develop their attachment to peers and to the school.

This chapter presents the results of individual OLS regression predicting an individual's bond to school as well as the effect that the social environment plays on the average school bond within a school. Table 3.1 provides the descriptive statistics for all variables in the analysis. The statistical analysis begins with Table 3.2 which provides the results of the OLS regression analysis for all 5th grade students. In order to test the additional hypotheses, the model had to be separated by gender and race to test the equivalency across models. These OLS results are also found in Table 3.2.

Table 3.3 provides the OLS regression results for the male-only and female-only samples with gender interaction effects. Table 3.4 introduces the separate OLS regression models predicting school bonding for whites and African Americans with the interaction effects of race.[43]

Finally, Table 3.5 provides the hierarchical linear model assessing the effect of the school context on the average student-school bond relationship. This model will test the school-level hypotheses posed in the previous chapter, including the interaction of the school-level variables on the mean effect of the level-1 predictors within a school.

The 5th grade sample

This 5th grade sample consisted of 5,865 students. The average age of the students in this sample was approximately 11 years old and the mean GPA was 3. 0. Approximately half (51 percent) of the respondents were male and a quarter (25 percent) classified themselves as African American and roughly 8 percent reported being a Non-African American minority. Approximately 70 percent of the students indicated they come from an intact home where they reside with two parents. Finally, only a third of the students (32 percent) reported being in a physical fight during the present academic year.

The findings of the OLS regression model predicting school bonding among a 5th grade population are presented in Table 3. 2 (all 5th).[45] The model examined the effect of the demographic variables, the family variables, individual grade point average, and delinquency variables.

This model was able to explain roughly 3 percent in the variation in school bonding among 5th grade students. Six variables were found to be significant; gender, being Non-African American, family structure, and delinquent peer associations were significant at the $p < 0.001$ level. The effect of being African American and age were significant at the $p < 0.05$ level. The standardized regression coefficients suggest that the strongest predictor of school bonding is delinquent peer associations.

Association with delinquent peers, found to be the strongest predictor of a student's school bond, significantly reduced one's bond to school. At this age, children are in the early stages of developing attachments to their peer group. Lending support to the initial hypothesis, this finding indicates that students who associate with a delinquent peer group exhibit lower levels of school bonding as early as the 5th grade.

Table 3. 1: Descriptive Statistics for 5th grade Public Schools and Students in a Mid Atlantic State.

Variable	Mean	Std. Dev.	Min	Max
Individual Level				
School Bond	10.17	1.27	7.00	16.00
Age	10.63	0.60	9.00	11.00
Sex	0.51	0.50	0.00	1.00
African American	0.25	0.44	0.00	1.00
Non-African American Minority	0.08	0.21	0.00	1.00
Grade Point Average	3.03	0.84	0.00	4.00
Lives with two parents	0.71	0.46	0.00	1.00
Association With Delinquent Peers	5.70	0.68	3.00	7.00
Drug Use	13.66	2.55	1.00	27.00
Has been in Fight this year	0.32	0.47	0.00	1.00

Table 3. 1: Descriptive Statistics for 5th grade Public Schools and Students in a Mid Atlantic State (cont.).

Variable	Mean	Std. Dev.	Min	Max
School Level				
School Enrollment	642.93	236.46	299.00	1214.00
Ability Grouping	0.47	0.50	0.00	1.00
Free and Reduced Lunch	40.91	13.31	0.00	65.80
Minority Enrollment	41.13	17.56	3.90	96.10
Use of Punishment	5.24	4.69	0.40	29.30
School Fighting	0.32	0.01	0.17	0.50
School Drug Use	13.69	0.36	13.20	14.70

Student N= 5503; School N= 43

Table 3.2: Unstandardized and (Standardized) Regression Coefficients Predicting School Bonding Among 5th Grade Public School Students.[44]

Variable	All 5th	Coefficient (beta) 5th Gender		5th Race		
		Male	Female	White	African American	Non-African American Minority
Constant	10.69	10.97	10.81	10.65	11.26	11.40
Male	0.10*** (0.04)			0.13***	0.09	0.03
African American	0.08* (0.03)	0.11	0.08			
Non-African American Minority	0.18*** (0.04)	0.14	0.21***			
Age	0.06* (0.03)	0.05	0.08*	0.07	0.04	0.06
Living with Both Parents	0.16*** (0.06)	0.08	0.24***	0.18***	0.17*	-0.07
Grade Point Average	-0.00 (-0.00)	-0.01	0.01	0.01	-0.00	-0.03
Drug Use	-0.01 (-0.01)	-0.00	-0.02*	0.00	0.02	-0.01
Fighting	-0.03 (-0.01)	-0.01	0.07	-0.00	0.09	0.05
Association with Delinquent Peers	-0.25*** (-0.13)	-0.20***	-0.30***	-0.22***	-0.28***	-0.27***
Adjusted R-Square	0.03	0.01	0.04	0.02	0.03	0.01
Sample Size (N)	5503	2786	2717	3556	1484	463

Family structure was found to be the next strongest predictor in the model. Those students who report living with two parents have higher levels of school bonds than those who come from a household with only one parent or where a step-parent is present or those who do not live with either parent. This is a result that supports the initial hypothesis that a traditional, 'intact' family would have a positive effect on the school bond. As previously mentioned, during elementary school children are still very attached to their parents. In most cases, when a student's parents are married, there is less of a chance that the student will get mixed signals regarding the importance of education that may occur when the managing life between parents in separate households. Thus, residing with both biological parents is a significant and strong predictor of a 5th graders bond to school.

Age was also found to be a significant predictor of school bonding, however not in the hypothesized direction. The older students in the class experienced higher levels of school bonding than those who were younger. Again, individual development may help to explain this finding. Those students who are the youngest in the class are still more attached to their parents than their peers or the school. These young students are developmentally behind the older students who have already begun to distance themselves from parents and towards peers.

Again, this finding is contrary to the initial hypothesis suggesting that older students would experience lower levels of bonding. The initial hypothesis was developed with the thought that older students in a class have experienced educational or behavioral difficulties which held them back a year from their peer group. It is interesting to note that this situation may actually increase the student-school bond in the early stages of education.

While students may be held back from their initial peer group, they are still developmentally attached to their parents more so than their peers. As such, the separation from one peer group can be easily overcome with the introduction of another peer group.

At the same time, parents may make the choice to postpone their child's entrance into the school (kindergarten or pre-K) to allow their child to mature one more year and be better prepared for the school setting. These children have had an additional year of development towards adolescence and preparation for the school experience. Since these children are a bit more mature than they would have been a year previous, it is possible they may also pose less of a problem to teachers again fostering a more pro-social bond with the school personnel than may have been the case were they to have started before they were ready.

Being male was also found to significantly increase one's bond to school. This finding is counter to the initial hypothesis and ascertation by Cohen (1955) that grade school boys have difficulty identifying with female teachers and administrators. It was initially thought that males, more so than females, are likely to exert their independence thus experiencing lower levels of school attachment. Boys may simply develop an attachment to school, or at least the attachment is more salient, at an earlier age than females. During this early stage of development, girls are more closely bonded to their parents than boys, thus boys have more independence to begin fostering social bonds outside the family unit.

Finally, being African American and Non-African American minority was found to significantly increase a student's bond to school. This finding was contrary to the initial hypothesis and findings from Cernkovich and Giordano (1992) suggesting that African American students would experience lower levels of school bonding than their white counterparts. It is also thought that Non-African American minorities would experience lower levels of school bonding than their white peers.

It is difficult to explain why 5th grade African American and Non-African American minority students would experience a higher level of school bonding than their counterparts. It is possible that school is a safety zone for these students who may come from dangerous neighborhoods where they may not feel safe. Children who come from disorganized or dangerous areas may look to school, even in the early years, as a peaceful haven away from the chaos that surrounds their everyday life. Particularly in the inner city areas, African Americans and Latinos (a large component of the Non-African American minority sample) comprise a majority of the population residing in these transitional or disorganized neighborhoods.

One part of these transitional neighborhoods in this state is migrant populations, the majority of which are of Hispanic descent. The effect of being Non-African American minority was noted as one of the strongest in the model. It is possible that at this young age these children, who may be getting acclimated to a new environment, may find school to be a stable setting providing interaction with peers they may be missing in a new location.

Counter to the initial hypotheses, neither individual drug use nor individual delinquency was found to have a significant effect on the school bond. It is interesting to note that individual delinquency and drug use were not found to be significant predictors of the school bond. Previous research has continuously found evidence of the relationship between delinquency, including drug use, and school bonding. Research has indicated a negative correlation between pro-social bonding and individual delinquency and drug use. While previous research provides support for the initial hypotheses, little has dealt with the issue in a grade school population.

While it is possible that 5th grade students are not engaging in high rates of delinquency or drug use, it may be more likely that measure is biased. It is possible that the behavior of these children is still highly monitored by parents, teachers, and guardians so that they do not have a great deal of unsupervised leisure time and when they misbehave it is usually punished. When behavior is monitored, individuals are less likely to engage in delinquent behavior and particularly drug use. At the same time, however, there has been literature suggesting that children in elementary school are acting in a delinquent manner; the behavior is simply not captured by traditional survey questions.

In this particular instance, the individual delinquency measure consists of a yes, no question regarding physical fighting. Developmental psychologists may argue that this variable is male specific. A question regarding physical aggression alienates the female population since young females act in a more passive aggressive rather than physically aggressive manner. Thus, the measure of delinquency for this 5th grade sample is actually only measuring male aggression rather than 5th grade delinquency.

Further, grade point average was not found to have a significant impact on the student-school bond. At this age, grade point average may not be as important of predictor of a student's commitment to school. While it is thought that students who are academically successful are less likely to engage in delinquency and are thus more bonded, these findings do not support such a statement. Grades may not be relevant to the elementary school bond. Instead, a school bond may have more to do with the student's level of comfort in the school environment. As such, the impact of an individual-level variable (such as GPA) on the school bond may actually depend on the school context. This will be analyzed further in the HLM results (Table 3.5).

Gender and School Bonds

To further understand the difference between the male school bond and female school bond, the sample was split by gender group and the same analysis was run for each gender specific model. A Chow test was conducted to determine that there was in fact a significant difference between the gender groups ($F=768.377$; $p=0.001$).[46] This finding indicated that the models estimating school bonding in the 5th grade are not equivalent across gender groups.

Table 3.2 (5th Gender) also presents the results of the OLS regression for males and females respectively. The model indicates that approximately 5 percent of the variation in female school bonds and roughly 2 percent of the variation in male school bonding can be explained by the variables in this analysis. Age, being Non-African American, parent's marital status, individual drug use, and delinquent peer associations were found to be significant for females, while the only significant predictor of school bonding among males was association with delinquent peers.

Association with delinquent peers significantly reduced one's bond to school for both males and females, though the effect was larger for females than for males. The female model, however, produced additional significant results. Older 5th grade girls experience a higher level of school bonding. Non-African American minority females experience a higher level of school bonding than white or African American females. Girls who come from a two-parent home experience higher levels of school bonding. Finally, individual drug use significantly increased a female's bond to school. Though this was not a strong effect, it further differentiated the male and female model of school bonding.

Further testing the differences in these effects, Table 3.3 presents the results of interaction between gender and those variables found to produce different effects between the sexes; namely being Non-African American, family structure, drug use, and association with delinquent peers. These four variables were created to test for significant differences in the effect of the aforementioned variables on the school bond across genders.

Three of the four interaction effects were found to be significant. That is to say that the effects of living with two parents, individual drug use, and association with delinquent peers significantly differ between the sexes. The effect of being Non-African American minority, however, was not found to significantly differ between males and females.   The effect of living with both biological parents and individual drug use was found to be lower for males than females, while the effect of delinquent peer association was found to have a smaller negative impact on the bond to school compared to a female's bond.

As previously noted, females tend to be more closely monitored by parents.   While supervision does not equate to a close relationship, residing with both parents at a point when females are still closely bonded with parents may improve the ability of parents to transmit values to their children.   Since males fight for independence at an earlier age, the impact of family structure may very well have a stronger effect on a females' ability to develop prosocial bonds to her school.

Further, behavioral expectations for boys and girls at this age are still somewhat gender specific.   Boys experience a different range of acceptable behaviors than do girls.   The idea that boys are 'rough' while girls are 'gentle' is very much in place in the elementary school setting.   In part because this is the level at which the school system takes over the responsibility of socialization for American children. Students are continuing to associate with peer groups and as previously mentioned, males are beginning to exert their independence, finding peers increasingly salient in their life.   As these boys settle into peer groups, the school environment continues to foster traditional gender role expectations.   That is to say, teachers are less likely to respond when a group of boys are 'roughhousing' on the playground than when the same behavior is exhibited by a group of girls.   Thus, association with delinquent peers is more destructive to the female school bond than the male's bond to school.

One of the most interesting findings is the differential effect of drug use between genders.   Particularly at such a young age it is puzzling to note that individual drug use was significant for females and not so for males.

These results suggest that when a girl is delinquent (by using drugs) or has delinquent peers, the school bond is affected. Delinquency and delinquent peer associations are more destructive of the female school bond than the male school bond.   Traditional gender roles, like the middle class value structure, can be pervasive in the public school system.   There are behavioral expectations in the school system that allows boys to be a bit more mischievous in their behavior than girls.   When a boy acts out or hangs out with a delinquent peer group, teachers or school administrators may be less likely to punish behavior, passing it off as 'boys will be boys'. When girls experiment with drugs or associates with a rough crowd, it is thought to be more improper and may be more likely to evoke punishment or at least a response by teachers and school administrators. If these girls are experiencing punishment in the school or isolation from teacher or administrators based on their delinquent behavior or peer group, bonding to school becomes more difficult for girls. Thus, delinquency and association with delinquent peers is more strongly associated with the school bond among girls.

Race and School Bonds

The initial model indicated that being African American or a Non-African American minority actually increases a 5th grader's bond to school. While the effect of race was found to be significant in the full model, it begs the question about equality of models across race categories. In order to test the equivalency of models, a separate model was run for African Americans, Non-African American minorities and Whites. Table 3. 2 also presents the results of the regression predicting school bonding for the White-only, African American-only and Non-African American-only samples. The Chow Test was then conducted to determine the equivalency between models.

The Chow test indicated significant differences between the models. Specifically, the African American model was not equivalent to the White model ($F = 1671. 63$; $p > 0. 001$), the Non-African American model was not equivalent to the White model ($F = 1701. 98$; $p > 0. 001$), and finally the African American model was not equivalent to the Non-African American minority model ($F = 2293. 16$; $p > 0. 001$).

As indicated by the Chow test, the model predicting school bonds were not equivalent between race/ethnic categories. The race/ethnic specific models were not found to explain a high proportion of variation in school bonding. The complete model was found to explain approximately 1 percent of the variation in school bonding for Non-African American minorities, 2 percent of the variation in school bonding for White students and approximately 3 percent for African American students.

Table 3.3: Regression Coefficients Predicting School Bonding Among 5th Grade Public School Students With Gender Interaction.[47,48]

Variable	Model 1	Model 2	Coefficient (beta) Model 3	Model 4	Model 5
Constant	10.69	12.78	12.85	12.57	13.21
Male	0.10*** (0.04)	0.07 (0.03)	-0.06 (-0.03)	0.44* (0.18)	-0.69* (-0.27)
African American	0.08* (0.03)	0.10* (0.03)	0.10* (0.03)	0.10* (0.03)	0.10* (0.03)
Non-African American Minority	0.18*** (0.04)	0.20*** (0.05)	0.17*** (0.05)	0.17*** (0.05)	0.17*** (0.05)
Age	0.06* (0.03)	0.04 (0.02)	0.04 (0.02)	0.04 (0.02)	0.04 (0.02)
Living with Both Parents	0.16*** (0.06)	0.14*** (0.04)	0.23*** (0.08)	0.14*** (0.05)	0.14*** (0.05)
Grade Point Average	-0.00 (-0.00)	-0.00 (-0.00)	-0.00 (-0.00)	-0.00 (-0.00)	-0.00 (-0.00)
Drug Use	-0.01 (-0.01)	0.00 (0.01)	0.01 (0.01)	0.02* (0.04)	-0.00 (-0.01)
Delinquency	-0.03 (-0.01)	-0.12*** (-0.12)	-0.12*** (-0.12)	-0.13*** (-0.12)	-0.13*** (-0.12)
Association with Delinquent Peers	-0.25*** (-0.13)	-0.16*** (-0.08)	-0.16*** (-0.08)	-0.25*** (-0.13)	-0.23*** (-0.12)
Male* Non-African American		-0.05 (-0.01)			
Male* Parents			-0.18* (-0.07)		
Male* Drugs				-0.03* (-0.16)	
Male* Delinquent Peers					0.13** (0.29)
Adjusted R-Square	0.03	0.04	0.04	0.04	0.04

Both the White-only and African American-only models indicate that coming from a two-parent household is a significant predictor of school bonding. The same was not true for Non-African American minorities. In addition, being male significantly improves the school bond in the White-only sample, but not for African American or Non-African American minorities.

The one effect found to be significant for all three race/ethnic groups was that of delinquent peer association. Delinquent peer associations significantly reduce a student's bond to school regardless of race/ethnic background. The importance of peers transcends race/ethnic classification. If a child associates with a peer group which is involved in delinquency, this association will negatively affect the child's bond to school. As stated earlier in the literature review, delinquency and delinquent peer groups exhibit a normative structure that is counter to what is expected in American public schools. This value conflict has been hypothesized to weaken the student's bond to school.

Age, Grade point average, drug use and fighting were not found to be significant in any of the 3 race/ethnic models. It is not surprising to note grade point average, drug use and fighting are not significant across racial models, particularly when these variables are not found to be significant in the combined model. Age, however, is not a salient factor in predicting the school bond by race/ethnicity.

Noting the difference in the African American-, Non-African American minority- and White-only models, another regression was run to test for the significant differences in the effects of these variables on school bonding between the race/ethnic groups. Three interaction terms were created to test the effect of gender and age across the race/ethnic categories. Table 3.4 provides the results of the 5th grade OLS regression with interaction terms for race/ethnicity.

None of these interaction terms were found to be significant. Thus, while gender was significant in the White-only model, and not the African American or Non-African American minority models the interaction terms indicate that these effects were not significantly different across race/ethnic groups.

Further, coming from a two-parent household was found to significantly improve the African American and White bond to school, though the same was not true for Non-African American minorities. The interaction terms, however indicates that the effect of a two-parent household does not significantly differ across race/ethnic categories.

Table 3.4: Regression Coefficients Predicting School Bonding Among 5th Grade Public School Students with Race Interaction.[49,50]

Variable			Coefficient (beta)				
			Model 1	Model 2	Model 3	Model 4	Model 5
Constant			10.69	12.78	12.78	12.78	12.78
Male			0.10*** (0.04)	0.01 (0.02)	0.07 (0.03)	0.06 (0.03)	0.06 (0.02)
African American			0.08* (0.03)	0.01 (0.03)	0.10* (0.03)	0.08* (0.03)	0.10* (0.03)
Non-African American Minority			0.18 (0.04)	0.17 (0.05)	0.20*** (0.05)	0.08 (0.04)	0.11 (0.03)
Age			0.06* (0.03)	0.07* (0.03)	0.04 (0.02)	0.04 (0.02)	0.04 (0.02)
Living with Both Parents			0.16*** (0.06)	0.14*** (0.05)	0.14*** (0.04)	0.14*** (0.05)	0.15*** (0.06)
Grade Point Average			-0.00 (-0.00)	-0.00 (-0.00)	-0.00 (-0.00)	-0.00 (-0.00)	-0.00 (-0.00)
Drug Use			-0.01 (-0.01)	-0.00 (-0.01)	0.00 (0.01)	0.00 (0.01)	0.00 (0.01)
Fighting			-0.03 (-0.01)	-0.12*** (-0.11)	-0.12*** (-0.12)	-0.13*** (-0.12)	-0.13*** (-0.12)
Association with Delinquent Peers			-0.25*** (-0.13)	-0.16*** (-0.08)	-0.16*** (-0.08)	-0.16*** (-0.08)	-0.16*** (-0.08)
African American* Male				-0.00 (-0.00)			
Non-African American * Male					-0.05 (-0.01)		
African American * Living with Both Parents						-0.03 (-0.01)	
Non-African American minority* Living with Both Parents							0.09 (0.02)
Adjusted R-Square			0.03	0.04	0.04	0.04	0.04

Summary of Regression Results

In short, the strongest predictor of school bonding among 5th grade students is one's peer group. When students associate with delinquent peers they experience lower levels of school bonding. This is true of both males and females as well as across all race/ethnic categories. However, the gender specific models indicate that delinquent peer associations, as well as drug use, are more detrimental to the female school bond than the male school bond.

Family structure was also found to play a significant role in school bonding for White and African American students, but not so for Non-African American minorities. Family structure was found to be the second strongest predictor of school boding overall, and significantly improves the school bond for females.

While the school bond is thought to be an individual experience, only a small proportion of variation is explained by the measured individual level variables. Within a school, students are influenced by the context in which they learn. Therefore, it is possible that school context may help to model the student-school bond relationship.

School Bonds and the School Context

One of the unique components of this research is the focus on the school-level variables in predicting a student's social bond to school. This is of particular interest since recent high profile acts of school violence have brought into question the school bonding aspect of the school context. This research asks the question if the school itself can impact a student's fondness or affinity for the teachers, administrators, and a pride in the school itself.

The social development model suggests that prosocial attachments act as protective factors against delinquent behavior, and schools have the ability to assist in the development of such attachments. The schools can provide students with school related activities, a measure of discipline to affirm appropriate behaviors, and also provide a nurturing environment where students feel comfortable to learn and excel.

The school-level measures in this analysis are utilized to asses if the school context can significantly impact the mean level of bonding within a school. Further, the mean effect of an individual-level variable on school bonding could depend upon the school context as estimated by school-level measures. The measures employed, such as use of ability grouping, proportion of students in poverty, school enrollment and proportion of minorities enrolled, speak to the importance of a comfortable school environment where students can learn and excel. There is also a measure of proportion of students disciplined in the school to assess the impact of punishment and school control on the school bond. Finally, there are school-level measures of delinquency and drug use which will test the impact of the school climate and the learning environment in which these students are expected to be comfortable and productive.

5th Grade School- Level Effects

Table 3.5 presents the results of HLM analysis. The structure of the table reflects the estimated fixed effects of the school-level variables effect on each possible level-1 (individual-level) outcome.[51] These school variables can have either a direct effect on the mean level of the school bond within a school or it can moderate the effect of a level-1 variable on the school bond. Thus, an individual-level effect may depend on the level of a school variable.

The average score on the school bonding scale for students in the 5th grade was 5.156 which ranged from 0 to 8. The interclass correlations indicate that approximately 2 percent of the variation in school bonds among 5th grade students can be explained by between school effects. This is not a sizable proportion of explained variation and indicates that the school context has very limited explanatory power modeling the student-school bond. While the low proportion of explained variation would suggest HLM estimation would have limited utility, it was important to use the technique if only for exploratory purposes.

The school level variables produced no significant impact on the mean level of school bonding while controlling for all the other individual level variables in the model. In other words, the use of ability grouping, school enrollment, proportion of minorities enrolled, proportion of students punished, proportion of students disciplined, the mean level of delinquency in the school, or the mean level of drug use in a school did not significantly impact the mean level of school bonding between 5th grade schools.

Not surprisingly, the same non-significant results were found for most level-2 (school-level) outcomes. The school-level variables did not have a significant moderating effect on 5th grade average male's school bond, an average non-African American minority's school bond, an average student who come from a two-parent home, the average student who associate with delinquent peers, the average student who is above the mean age of their classroom and the average student who engages in an above average amount of delinquency. School-level variables also had no moderating effect on the impact of GPA on school bonding.

The average African American bond to school was found to be depended on the proportion of minorities enrolled at his or her school (see Table 3.5; African American), as well as on the proportion of disciple exacted in his or her school. Further, those students who use drugs experience more alienation when they attend schools with a low level of drug use among students (See Table 3. 5; Drug Use).

In the 5th grade, schools that enrolled an above average proportion of minority students increased an African American student's level of school bonding. In other words, African American students experience higher levels of school bonding in schools which enroll a larger proportion of minority students. This finding supports the initial hypothesis, suggesting that students are more comfortable in a school environment that surrounds them with people more like themselves.

In addition, African American students experience lower levels of bonding to their school when that school exacts discipline on an above average proportion of students. In other words, there is a significant decline in the mean level of school bonding for African American students when the school hands out an above average number of suspensions, expulsions, and zero tolerance expulsions. This is not surprising given the research findings that minority students are disproportionately punished in the American public school system. Research has indicated that African American students feel targeted by the school when it comes to discipline. When students perceive they are targets it is rational to believe they would withdraw from school leading to a reduction in the school bond.

Finally, the negative impact on individual drug use on the school bond depends upon the mean level of drug use in a school. An individual's drug use is more harmful to his or her school bond when attending a school with below average drug use. The more drug use in a school, the more acceptance of substance use, and thus the lower the negative impact on the school bond. Again, this finding supports the initial hypothesis indicating that when drugs are more readily available in the school or if the climate among a student's peers is accepting of drug use, the negative impact on such behavior will be lower than in an environment where drug use remains less accepted.

Though the 5th grade HLM model did not produce a sizeable proportion of explained variation between schools, the findings, in regards to the impact of the school context on students, indicate that at the elementary school bond is fostered when students are with other students that are like themselves. Whether it is an African American who exhibits a stronger bond to a school with a larger minority population, or the drug using students experiencing less of a deleterious effect on his or her bond to school when enrolled in a school with high drug use, a students bond to school is improved (even when he/she is delinquent) when they are in a school with other students who look or behave like themselves.

The contextual variables employed in the HLM analysis provided little additional understanding of the school bond. The results of the HLM analysis suggest that the school bond is an individual phenomenon. That is to say the school context does not significantly improve one's understanding of the school bond. Thus, future research should focus on the individual characteristics of students to better understand the school bond among 5th grade students.

Summary of 5th grade results

In summary, results from Table 3.2 suggest that there are six significant predictors of school bonds among 5th grade students. Older students experience higher levels of bonding to school, contradicting the original hypothesis that students who are around the average age for their grade experience a stronger bond to school. Family structure was also found to be a significant predictor of school bonding. Those students who reside in a two-parent home have a stronger bond to school than those students who do not reside with two parents, supporting the initial hypothesis that coming from an intact family unit would increase an individual's bond to school.

The strongest predictor of school bonding among 5th grade students was association with delinquent peers. Students who report association with delinquent peers had significantly lower levels of school bonding. This supports the initial research hypothesis. Finally, contrary to the original hypothesis, males, Non-African American minorities and African Americans were found to have a higher level of school bonding.

Table 3.5: Estimated Effects of School Context on the 5th Grade School Bond.

Outcome	Parameter		Coefficient
Intercept			
	Intercept,	G00	9.29***
	Ability Group	G01	-0.76
	Enrollment	G02	-0.00
	Minority	G03	0.01
	Poverty	G04	-0.01
	Punished	G05	0.05
	Drug Use	G06	-1.24
	Fighting	G07	1.33
Male			
	Intercept	G10	0.35
	Ability Group	G11	-0.00
	Enrollment	G12	-0.00
	Minority	G13	0.00
	Poverty	G14	0.00
	Punished	G15	-0.00
	Drug Use	G16	0.17
	Fighting	G17	-0.64
African American			
	Intercept	G20	0.32
	Ability Group	G21	-0.01
	Enrollment	G22	-0.00
	Minority	G23	0.01*
	Poverty	G24	0.01
	Punished	G25	-0.01*
	Drug Use	G26	0.16
	Fighting	G27	-0.68

Table 3.5: Estimated Effects of School Context on the 5th Grade School
Bond. (Cont.)

Outcome	Parameter		Coefficient
Non-African American Minority			
	Intercept	G30	-0.52
	Ability Group	G31	0.11
	Enrollment	G32	0.00
	Minority	G33	0.00
	Poverty	G34	-0.01
	Punished	G35	0.00
	Drug Use	G36	-0.14
	Fighting	G37	0.74
Living with Both Parents			
	Intercept	G40	-0.01
	Ability Group	G41	0.07
	Enrollment	G42	0.00
	Minority	G43	-0.00
	Poverty	G44	0.00
	Punished	G45	0.00
	Drug Use	G46	0.03
	Fighting	G47	0.08
Age			
	Intercept	G50	0.08
	Ability Group	G51	0.07
	Enrollment	G52	-0.00
	Minority	G53	-0.00
	Poverty	G54	0.00
	Punishment	G55	-0.00
	Drug Use	G56	0.12
	Fighting	G57	-0.19

Table 3.5: Estimated Effects of School Context on the 5th Grade School Bond. (Cont.)

Outcome	Parameter		Coefficient
Grade Point Average			
	Intercept	G60	0.09
	Ability Group	G61	-0.00
	Enrollment	G62	0.00
	Minority	G63	-0.00
	Poverty	G64	-0.00
	Punished	G65	-0.00
	Drug Use	G66	0.01
	Fighting	G67	0.31
Individual Drug Use			
	Intercept	G70	0.03
	Ability Group	G71	0.03
	Enrollment	G72	0.00
	Minority	G73	0.00
	Poverty	G74	-0.00
	Punished	G75	-0.00
	Drug Use	G77	-0.14
Fighting			
	Intercept	G80	0.12
	Ability Group	G81	-0.13
	Enrollment	G82	0.00
	Minority	G83	-0.00
	Poverty	G84	-0.00
	Punished	G85	0.15
	Drug Use	G86	-0.17
	Fighting	G87	0.09
Association with Delinquent Peers			
	Intercept	G90	-0.09
	Ability Group	G91	0.08
	Enrollment	G92	0.00
	Minority	G93	0.00
	Poverty	G94	0.00
	Punished	G95	-0.00
	Drug Use	G96	-0.02
	Fighting	G97	-0.55

The Chow test indicated significant differences in the slopes of the gender- and race-specific models, so an additional set of regressions were completed to survey these potential differences. While it was noted that the effect of family structure, drug use, and delinquent peer associations significantly differed between males and females, no individual effects were found to significantly differ between Whites and African Americans.

Contextual variables describing the school environment produced little significant effect on the student-school bond relationship. No school level measures had a significant overall effect on the average student-school bond relationship. There were however a few significant interaction effects. Students who use drugs experience a weaker deleterious effect on the school bond when they attend schools were drug use is more common. African American students who attend schools with a higher proportion of other African American students experience a stronger bond to school; though, this school bond is weakened when African Americans attend schools which exact discipline on a higher proportion of students.

In short, contextual variables of the school environment do not significantly influence the school bond. Rather, the school bond is an individual phenomenon suggesting that individual factors impact the development of a student's prosocial bond to school rather than the context of the school itself.

Chapter 4

The Social Bond in Middle School

The transition from elementary school to middle school is noted as one of the most difficult times in adolescent development. These children are developing stronger bonds to their peers and distancing themselves from their parents and family. In addition, the school becomes a place of learning and of activity. Many middle schools provide extracurricular activities and avenues for students to socialize and bond outside of the classroom. Not all students have a smooth transition from elementary to high school. Those who have difficulty during this transition experience discipline problems in the home and in school, school failure, and exhibit behaviors identified with withdrawing from the school or the educational experience.

The following analysis looks at the impact of individual-level and contextual school-level variables on the student-school bond in the 8th grade. Table 4.1 presents descriptive statistics for all variables in the analysis. Table 4.2 presents the OLS regression model predicting school bonding, followed by the model for males and females as well as school bonding models separated by race/ethnic categories. Table 4.3 presents the results of an OLS regression with gender interaction followed by Table 4.4 which provides results of race/ethnicity interactions. Finally, Table 4.5 provides the results of the Hierarchical Linear Model which examines the impact of the school context on the mean level of school bonding found within and between middle schools.

Sample Descriptives

Table 4.1 displays the means and standard deviations for the 8th grade sample. The average age of the sample was approximately 14 years old. Approximately 51 percent of the respondents were male and 55 percent of the students came from a home with both parents present. While over 60 percent of the sample was White, 32 percent of the respondents classified themselves as African American and 7 percent of the respondents were of a Non-African American minority.

The means of the school variables indicate approximately 52 percent of the schools employ ability grouping. In other words, over half of the schools separate the 8th grade class by ability in primarily English and Math. The average enrollment of the middle school sample was 755 students, with approximately 37 percent minority enrollment and 23 percent receiving free or reduced lunch.

8th Grade Individual Level Effects

Table 4.2 presents the results of the regression model predicting the 8th grade student-school social bond from individual level variables. This model examined the effect of the demographic variables, family structure, individual grade point average, mean level of parental education and delinquency variables. This model indicates that 19 percent of the variation in school bonds can be explained by these variables. Eight variables were found to be significant: age, gender, family structure, parent's education, GPA, drug use, delinquency and delinquent peer associations.

The standardized regression coefficients suggest that one of the strongest predictors of school bonding in the 8th grade is grade point average (beta= 0.15). Students with higher GPA's have higher levels of school bonds. This finding supports the initial hypothesis that students with higher GPA's will experience a higher level of bond to the school. In part the GPA is an extension of one component of the school bond, commitment. If students are committed to school, it is likely that they will achieve higher grades than those students who are not as committed. While there are differing types of involvement in a school, it is feasible that those students with higher GPA's will also place a higher value on involvement in school activities. Thus, it is no surprise a high GPA significantly predicts one's bond to school.

Table 4.1: Descriptive Statistics for 8th grade Public School and School Students in a Mid Atlantic State.[52]

Variable	Mean	St.Dev.	Minimum	Maximum
Individual-Level				
School Bond	28.54	6.17	7.00	43.00
Age	13.75	0.65	13.00	16.00
Male	0.51	0.50	0.00	1.00
African American	0.32	0.43	0.00	1.00
Non-African American Minority	0.07	0.34	0.00	1.00
Grade Point Average	2.68	0.93	1.00	4.00
Lives with both Parents	0.55	0.49	0.00	1.00
Parent's Education	12.77	4.08	0.00	18.00
Association With Delinquent Peers	18.74	6.87	1.00	45.00
Drug Use	16.52	5.75	1.00	88.00
Delinqueny	14.64	7.46	0.00	63.00

Table 4.1: Descriptive Statistics for 8th grade Public School and School Students in a Mid Atlantic State (cont.).[52]

Variable	Mean	St.Dev.	Minimum	Maximum
School-Level				
School Enrollment	755.29	256.30	167.00	1214.00
Ability Grouping	0.51	0.50	0.00	1.00
Free and Reduced Lunch	36.96	9.78	11.96	54.40
Minority Enrollment	38.82	11.85	14.35	70.47
Use of Punishment	19.12	10.44	5.39	51.50
School Drug Use	16.62	0.87	15.21	18.99
School Delinquency	14.52	1.00	12.98	16.86

Table 4.2: Unstandardized and (Standardized) Regression Coefficients Predicting School Bonding Among 8th Grade Public School Students.[53]

| Variable | All 8th | Coefficient (beta) 8th Gender | | 8th Race | | |
		Male	Female	White	African American	Non-African American Minority
Constant	37.34	36.22	37.58	37.60	34.06	35.08
Male	-0.17*** (-0.11)			-0.21***	-0.07	-0.19***
African American	-0.05 (-0.03)	0.04	-0.15**			
Non-African American Minority	-0.05 (-0.02)	-0.01	-0.00			
Age	-0.06*** (-0.05)	-0.07***	-0.05*	-0.06**	-0.04	-0.10*
Living with Both Parents	0.10*** (0.06)	0.12***	0.06*	0.11***	0.11**	-0.01
Grade Point Average	0.12*** (0.15)	0.10***	0.14***	0.13***	0.10***	0.11***
Parent's Education	0.01*** (0.05)	0.01**	0.01**	0.01***	0.01	0.01
Drug Use	-0.00* (-0.04)	-0.00	-0.01*	-0.05	-0.01	0.03
Delinquency	-0.02*** (-0.18)	-0.02***	-0.02***	-0.02***	-0.01***	-0.03***
Association with Delinquent Peers	-0.02*** (-0.14)	-0.01***	-0.02***	-0.02***	-0.01**	-0.01*
Adjusted R-Square	0.19	0.15	0.23	0.23	0.09	0.19
Sample Size (N)	5136	2631	2505	3564	1232	340

Unlike in the 5th grade, 8th grade males experience lower levels of school bonding in the middle school environment. This finding supports the initial hypothesis, and supports assertions by Cohen (1955) that school-aged boys have trouble relating to teachers (primarily female teachers) and school administrators. Further, males at this age are more likely to participate in delinquent activities, which previous research has found to be negatively correlated with school bonding. Males also fight the mechanisms of social control in the school environment more so than females. Boys will test the limits of a teacher, principal, or staff member to see how far they can stretch the rules. This finding again reaffirms assertions by Cohen regarding teachers and administrators.

Males at this age also find it difficult to identify their teachers as role models. Boys today look up to professional athletes such as Michael Jordan or Tiger Woods, musicians and rappers such as Eminem, or heroic civil servants such as New York City Police (NYPD) or Fire Department (NYFD) more so than their teachers. As such, young boys act in a manner attributed to their favorite athlete or musician which may further impact their perception of the importance or insignificance of school.

Finally, males may also be more readily punished in the middle school environment. If these young boys are more likely to engage in delinquency or inappropriate behavior, it is probable they will be the one's experiencing a high proportion of the punishment in the school. If these boys feel they are unduly targeted for punishment, this may further isolate them from the school experience and weaken their bond to school.

Unlike in the 5th grade where older students were more bonded to the school, it was determined that the older students in the 8th grade were found to have lower levels of school bonding; lending support to the initial hypothesis. In part this could be due to the fact many of these older students may have faced failure in school in previous years. Age, in the elementary school context, improved a bond with school. An earlier discussion noted that an older student may not have only experienced academic failure; rather his or her parents may have waited to enroll him or her in school. This provided the child with an additional year to mature before entering the school environment. By the end of middle school, however, older students may be more likely to be those who have experienced school failure.

A student who was held back a year may resent his or her teacher or school administration for the stigma this caused. Further, those older students are no longer with their age-appropriate peer group, so participation in school activities may become less and less attractive. When students do not have a positive relationship with their teachers and school administration and do not engage in school activities to be involved in school, it is no wonder why they exhibit a lower level of school bonding.

Structure of a student's family also has an impact on the school bonding of 8th graders. Those students who reside with both their parents experience higher levels of school bonding. In addition, the mean level of parent's/ adult guardian's education found in the home also impacts a student's school bond. When the home is an environment that supports education and the importance of education, the student is more likely to experience higher levels of bonding to his or her school. As previous research indicates, the way in which parents influence their child's perception of education is through their own educational accomplishments. Thus, those parents who have achieved higher levels of education have children with a stronger bond to school than others.

Parents are leading by example in terms of the student-school bond. Parents may speak fondly of their old teachers, schools, or experience in school activities. As a child hears this from his/her parent, he/she is likely to want a similar experience and in turn will appreciate or foster relationships with his/her teachers and participate in more school activities.

Further, parents who are more educated can be more effective in helping their children navigate the educational system. In addition, these parents are more likely to provide resources, such as home computers, newspaper/magazine subscriptions, encyclopedias, and travel experiences, to ensure academic success. In short, students whose parents have higher levels of education, are more likely to have a greater level of cultural capital than those with less educated parents.

Finally, individual delinquency, association with delinquent peers, and substance use all significantly reduced one's bond to school. When students are involved in delinquent behavior, whether it is drug use or other forms of delinquency, they are less likely to be bonded to school. These behaviors are counter to the norms and values taught in the school. Therefore, the students are rebelling against the teaching of the school simply by their delinquent actions. When a student is engaged in delinquency, he or she spends less time on school work and is usually less attentive in class. Delinquency has also been found to be negatively correlated with GPA which was already noted to be a strong predictor of school bonding.

In addition, when one associates with a set of delinquent peers, he or she is part of a group with norms and values counter to what is expected in the school. Delinquent peers provide a student with an alternative set of values, which usually falls opposite of the prosocial values of the school. Thus, the greater the participation with delinquent peers, the lower the level of school bonding.

In short, the OLS model suggests that individual-level variables such as individual characteristics, family variables, and delinquency measures can explain nearly 20 percent of the variation in school bonds. All of these variables, with the exception of race/ethnicity, significantly affect an individual's bond to school.

Gender Differences in 8th Grade School Bonding

In order to test the additional gender specific hypotheses, the sample was split by gender and the same analysis was run on the gender specific models. The results of the Chow test indicate that there is a significant difference in the male and female models in the 8th grade population ($F=519.41$; $p= 0.001$). Table 4.2 also presents the results of the OLS regression for the female-only and male-only samples side by side.

The male model was able to explain 15 percent of the variation in school bonding, while the female model was able to explain 23 percent. For females and males alike; age, GPA, family structure and parent's education level were found to significantly impact the school bond.

The gender specific models differ in terms of race. The effect of being African American was found to significantly reduce a female's bond to school. African American females experience weaker bonds to school than White females, while race had no significant effect on the male bond to school. This may indicate a significant gender gap in the effect of being African American on one's school bond.

Delinquency and association with delinquent peers were found to diminish the student-school bond for males as well as females. Participation in delinquent behaviors such as stealing or fighting, as well as association with delinquent peers are significant barriers to the development of solid prosocial bonds to school for both males and females. While there were no gender specific hypotheses addressing this issue, these findings continue to support the possibility that delinquency can significantly influence an individual's social bond to school. However, individual drug use was found to significantly reduce the school bond for females but a similar effect was not found for males. This is a change from the 5th grade sample where drug use was found to significantly improve the school bond for girls. Further, the effect of delinquent peer associations was found to be larger for girls than boys. Suggesting there may be a significant gender gap in the effect of drug use and delinquent peer associations on the school bond.

To test for significant differences in the effects of the aforementioned variables on the school bond across genders, a set of interaction terms were created. The results of these analyses are presented in Table 4.3.

Since there was a noted difference in the effect of being African American on the males and females, an interaction term was created to test if the difference between the sexes was statistically significant. This interaction term was entered to the regression equation in Model 2 (Table 4.3). It was determined that there is a statistically significant difference in the effect of being African American on school bonding for males and females, specifically that African American males experience a significantly stronger bond to school than African American females.

Research on school bonding by Cernkovich and Giordano (1992) indicated that African American girls experience the lowest levels of school bonding as compared to White girls or boys and African American boys. This study, noting that African American females experience a weaker bond to school than African American males, supports Cernkovich and Giordano's findings.

One reason for this could be the interplay between an individual's racial identity and school connectedness. The educational setting can have an impact on an individual's sense of self, as an individual and membership of a racial group. Adolescent girls are beginning to invent themselves and trying to foster emerging identities. This may be particularly difficult in the face of a social context that is framed by race and gender. Research suggests that public school expectations for African American girls are lower than for White girls (Ward, 2002). If a student does not feel as if she is being taken seriously by her teachers or stereotypes are holding a teacher back from connecting with her, the student may feel disconnected from the school environment.

It is during adolescence, according to developmental psychologists, when girls begin to devalue themselves and publicly dissociate themselves from institutions that devalue them, such as schools (Gilligan, 1991). African American females may have a more difficult time 'doing school' than White females. African American girls may have a more difficult time employing strategies to successfully negotiate the school setting.

Girls who are successful at 'doing school' are considered to be 'good' girls and are practically invisible to teachers and administrators, those who are not as successful may experience conflict or be labeled as 'troublemakers' by these adults. In short, there are a number of factors that influence a middle school girl. The intersection of race and gender may be particularly salient for these girls as they develop their identity and negotiate their way though middle school.

Model 3 introduces an interaction term to test the significant differences in the effect of family structure on school bonding between males and females. Though family structure was found to be statistically significant for both genders in the male-only and female-only models, there was a notable difference in the effect sizes between the sexes. Thus, the interaction term between gender and parent's marital status was added to the model.

The gender difference in the effect of family structure on one's bond to school is not significant. This finding suggests both males and females experience higher levels of school bonding when they live with both parents. An interesting note here is that both boys and girls experience an increase in the school bond. The rebellion for males has seemed to subside for the greater good of one's education. Boys are not rebelling against their parents' wishes, rather they have received the message regarding the importance of education and have become committed, attached, and involved with their school. This finding indicates that the family environment, from which a student comes, is also important in the school bonding process and something that requires more in-depth research in the future.

Finally, an interaction term, measuring the difference in the effect of drug use on school bonding between the sexes, was added to the regression in Table 4.3, Model 4. It was noted that the effect of drug use on school bonding did in fact differ between the sexes. The effect of individual drug use was found to have a smaller negative impact on a male's bond to school compared to a female's bond.

While the initial finding suggested that individual drug use decreases an individual's bond to school, it should be noted that the predominant drugs used by 8th grade students are alcohol, marijuana, and prescription drugs without a prescription. With that in mind, one must first understand how these drugs play into the lives of these middle school girls.

Research has indicated that there is a greater stigma associated with female delinquency (see: Chesney-Lind, 1998). Girls who use drugs or alcohol are more likely to experience a stigma, or be labeled as a 'bad girl', than their male peers. While 'boys may be boys' and experiment with smoking, drugs and alcohol; a female participating in such behavior diverges from the traditional gender expectations that females be less risk seeking and experimental. Thus, in the school environment where traditional gender roles are taught and anticipated, it is likely that teachers, school administrators, and other students may punish or stigmatize female drug use more so than a male use. When girls experience this stigma, particularly from teachers, the connectedness or attachment a female may have experienced will weaken, resulting in a weakening of the school bond.

At the same time, however, given the cross-sectional nature of this data, it is possible that those girls who are using drugs are already disengaging from the academic experience. These girls who report using drugs may be doing so having already experienced a disconnect from school. The school bond may already be weak, and is not a protective factor preventing participation in drug use among these middle school females.

Further, association with delinquent peers was found to weaken the school bond for females more so than for males. Again, associating with a delinquent peer group may be more acceptable for middle school boys. When girls associate with a 'tough' or 'delinquent' crowd, they are engaging in behavior counter to their expected gender roles and may experience punishment or social stigmatization. However, since peer groups are becoming more salient in the lives of middle school students, it is possible that those eighth grade girls who have already begun to disengage from school are those who are likely to associate with delinquent peers. Again, limited by the cross-sectional nature of this data, directionality cannot be established.

Table 4.3: Regression Coefficients Predicting School Bonding Among 8th Grade Public School Students With Gender Interaction (N=5136).[54]

Variable	Model 1	Model 2	Coefficient (beta) Model 3	Model 4	Model 5
Constant	37.34	37.90	37.81	38.43	38.92
Male	-0.17*** (-0.11)	-0.24*** (-0.14)	-0.16*** (-0.11)	-0.38** (-0.25)	-0.39** (-0.25)
African American	-0.05 (-0.03)	-0.07 (-0.09)	-0.08 (-0.05)	-0.09*** (-0.05)	-0.05* (-0.03)
Non-African American Minority	-0.05 (-0.02)	-0.07 (-0.02)	-0.07 (-0.02)	-0.02 (-0.02)	-0.05 (-0.01)
Age	-0.06*** (-0.05)	-0.06*** (-0.05)	-0.06*** (-0.05)	-0.06*** (0.05)	-0.06*** (0.05)
Living with Both Parents	0.10*** (0.06)	0.10*** (0.06)	0.11*** (0.07)	0.10*** (0.06)	0.10*** (0.06)
Grade Point Average	0.12*** (0.15)	0.11*** (0.13)	0.11*** (0.13)	0.11*** (0.13)	0.13*** (0.14)
Parent's Education	0.01*** (0.05)	0.23*** (0.14)	0.22*** (0.14)	0.22*** (0.14)	0.23*** (0.14)
Drug Use	-0.00* (-0.04)	-0.01* (-0.04)	-0.01* (-0.01)	-0.01*** (-0.10)	-0.00*** (-0.04)
Delinquency	-0.02*** (-0.18)	-0.01*** (-0.14)	-0.02*** (-0.14)	-0.01*** (-0.14)	-0.02*** (-0.18)
Association with Delinquent Peers	-0.02*** (-0.14)	-0.02*** (-0.18)	-0.02*** (-0.18)	-0.02*** (-0.18)	-0.02*** (-0.20)
Male* African American		0.15** (0.05)			
Male* Parents			-0.01 (-0.01)		
Male* Drugs				0.01*** (0.15)	
Male * Delinquency					0.01*** (0.17)
Adjusted R-Square	0.19	0.20	0.20	0.21	0.21

In summary, the models predicting school bonds for 8th grade boys and girls are not equal in predicting school bonding as indicated by the Chow test. There are three significant differences between the models. First, the effect of being African American on the school bond differs between the sexes. African American males experience a significantly stronger bond to school than their female counterparts. Further, the effect of individual drug use on school bonding also differed between the sexes. Drug use and delinquent peer associations were found to further deteriorate the school bond for females.

Racial Differences in School Bonding for 8th Grade Students
The analysis of race to this point has provided interesting results. In the full model, counter to the initial hypothesis, being African American or Non-African American minority was found to have no significant impact on an individual's bond to school. However, when the models were split by gender, it was noted that African American females experience a significantly weaker bond to school than African American males. To better understand racial differences in school bonding, the models were split by their racial/ethnic classification and an analysis was run to determine the equivalence of models for Whites, African Americans, and Non-African American minorities.

The results of the Chow test indicate that there is a significant difference in the white and non-African American minority models in the 8th grade population (F= 6642.53; p<0.001), a significant difference between Whites and African Americans (F= 5897.73; p<0.001) and a significant difference between African Americans and Non-African American minorities (F=1243.78; p<0.001). Again, the OLS regression results for these race/ethnicity specific models can be found in Table 4.2.

The model for Whites, including demographic, family and delinquency variables, was able to explain 23 percent of the variation in school bonding. Further, 19 percent of the variation in Non-African American minority school bonding and 9 percent of the variation in the African American school bond can be explained by this set of demographic, family and delinquency variables.

Grade point average was found to be a universal predictor of school bonds, indicating that students with higher GPA's, regardless of race/ethnicity, experienced higher levels of school bonds.

The models did diverge, however. While family structure was found to be a significant predictor influencing school bonding for

Whites and African Americans, no such result was noted in the Non-African American minority population. Being male and being an older student in the class significantly reduce the school bond for Whites and Non-African American minorities; however, not so for African Americans. Further, parent's level of education was only found to be significant for the white population.

The effect of individual drug use was not found to be significant for any of the race/ethnic models; however the effect of delinquency and delinquent peer associations were both found to significantly reduce the school bond for all race/ethnic groups.

Table 4.4 presents the results of an additional analysis to test for significant differences in the effects of age, family structure and parent's education on the school bond across race/ethnic categories. As previously noted, there were four differences noted across the different racial/ethnic models. Specifically, it was noted that age was significant for the White and Non-African American models, it was not found to be significant for the African American model. Thus, to test if the effect of age on the school bond significantly differs across the racial/ethnic groups an interaction term was created and added to the total regression model. Other interaction terms were created to test for significant differences in the effect of parental levels of education and family structure across race/ethnic categories.

Results of this analysis indicate that the effect of age does not significantly differ across race/ethnic groups. Race did not significantly influence the age/school bond relationship, suggesting that the effect of age on the school bond is not impacted by a student's race/ethnicity.

While residing with both parents was found to significantly improve the school bond for 8th grade White and African American students, the effect of residing with both parents is significantly weaker for Non-African American minority students. The effect of parent's level of education was also found to significantly differ by race/ethnicity. While the size of the effect is the same for Non-African American minorities as compared to other race/ethnic groups, these results indicate that Non-African American minority students experience a lesser increase in their school bond when they have better educated parents.

The Chow test indicates that the models predicting school bonds for Whites, African Americans and Non-African American minorities were not equal. While there were some differences noted in the race/ethnic-specific models, further analysis found that the effect of age did not significantly differ between the race/ethnic groups. The effect of living with both parents was significantly weaker for Non-African American minorities. Further, parental education significantly differed between Non-African American minority students and others, though no considerable difference in strength was noted. In sum, the effect of family structure and parental education was found to significantly differ between Non-African American minorities and other race/ethnic groups. Overall, the effect of family structure and parent's education on one's school bond is significantly lower for Non-African American minorities than other race/ethnic groups.

8th Grade School- Level Effects

Table 4.5 presents the effects of the middle school context on levels of school bonding in the 8th grade. The variance in the intercept in the conditional model was found to be significant ($\tau=0.01$; df=29; $\chi^2 = 49.65$; p=0.01) and also below the unconditional model suggesting additional variation in the mean level of school bonding is explained by individual level predictors. The interclass correlation indicates approximately 7 percent of the variation in school bonding can be explained by between school differences. The following analysis will explore the impact of the school context on the school bond.

Table 4.5 presents the results of HLM analysis. This table addresses the direct and moderating effects of the school context on the school bond. The structure of the table reflects the effect of the school-level variables on each possible level-1 (individual-level) relationship.

The results for the model predicting an average level of school bonding across schools (Table 4.5; Intercept) suggests those schools with an above average proportion of minorities, and an above state average proportion of students on free and reduced lunch experience a greater mean level of prosocial bonds in the school.

Table 4.4: Regression Coefficients Predicting School Bonding Among 8th Grade Public School Students With Race Interaction (N=5136).[55]

Variable	Model 1	Model 2	Coeff. (beta) Model 3	Model 4	Model 5	Model 6	Model 7
Constant	37.36	38.36	37.28	37.38	37.38	38.56	39.63
Male	-0.17*** (-0.12)	-0.18*** (-0.11)	-0.17*** (-0.11)	-0.18*** (-0.11)	-0.17*** (-0.11)	-0.17*** (-0.11)	-0.18*** (-0.12)
African American	-0.05 (-0.03)	-0.86 (-0.47)	-0.05 (-0.03)	-0.04 (-0.02)	-0.05 (-0.03)	-0.04 (-0.03)	-0.08 (-0.04)
Non-African American Minority	-0.05 (-0.02)	-0.16 (-0.05)	-0.05 (-0.02)	-0.17 (-0.05)	-0.08 (-0.01)	0.02 (0.01)	-0.06 (-0.02)
Age	-0.06*** (-0.05)	-0.07*** (-0.06)	-0.07*** (-0.05)	-0.06*** (-0.05)	-0.07*** (-0.05)	-0.07*** (-0.06)	-0.08* (-0.08)
Living with Both Parents	0.10*** (0.06)	0.10*** (0.06)	0.10*** (0.06)	0.10*** (0.06)	0.10*** (0.06)	0.00 (0.01)	0.03 (0.02)
Grade Point Average	0.12*** (0.15)	0.11*** (0.13)	0.12*** (0.15)	0.11*** (0.13)	0.10*** (0.12)	0.10*** (0.12)	0.08* (0.09)
Parent's Education	0.01*** (0.05)	0.01*** (0.06)	0.01*** (0.05)	0.01*** (0.06)	0.01*** (0.05)	0.01*** (0.04)	0.01* (0.04)
Drug Use	-0.00* (-0.04)	-0.01* (-0.04)	-0.00* (-0.04)	-0.01* (-0.04)	-0.01* (-0.04)	-0.01* (-0.05)	-0.01 (-0.05)
Delinquency	-0.02*** (-0.18)	-0.02** (-0.14)	-0.02** (-0.18)	-0.01*** (-0.14)	-0.02*** (-0.18)	-0.02*** (-0.20)	-0.03*** (-0.29)

Variable	Model 1	Model 2	Model 3	Model 4	Model 5	Model 6	Model 7
Association with Delinquent Peers	-0.02*** (-0.14)	-0.02*** (-0.18)	-0.02*** (-0.14)	-0.02*** (-0.18)	-0.02*** (-0.14)	-0.01*** (-0.12)	-0.01*** (-0.12)
African American *Age		-0.06 (-0.03)					
African American * Parents			0.01 (0.00)				
African American * Par. Ed.				-0.00 (-0.03)			
Non-AA Minority * Age					0.02 (0.11)		
Non-AA Minority * Parents						-0.12** (-0.04)	
Non-AA Minority * Par. Ed.							-0.01* (-0.08)
Adjusted R-Square	0.19	0.20	0.19	0.20	0.19	0.16	0.17

However, when schools rank above the state average in the proportion of students punished in a given school or show larger than average enrollments, schools exhibit a reduction in the mean level of prosocial school bonding among the students. In short, middle schools with an above average proportion of African American and Non-African American minority students and an above average proportion of students in poverty should expect to have students that are more committed, more involved and attached to teachers and staff. When schools are large, or punish a great deal of students, the average level of school bonding among students is lower.

Schools with a higher proportion of minority students enrolled were found to experience higher average bonds. This finding is counter to the initial hypothesis, but was found to be significant after controlling for other variables such as punishment that are possibly correlated with minority enrollment. While previous research suggests that minority students experience a sense of disconnectedness in the academic environment since expectations are based in the White, middle class value structure, this finding suggests that higher minority schools experience a slightly higher average level of bonding. This finding could be unique to this particular state and the pattern of busing in the middle school.

In order to maintain diversity in the public schools, this particular state busses White, middle school students who reside in suburban neighborhoods into urban schools. These schools are the local or neighborhood schools to a predominantly minority population. So, it is likely that the school environment is one that is more comfortable and culturally sensitive to minority students, and facilitates their family involvement thus increasing the average school bond.

These findings also indicate that schools with a high proportion of students in poverty may be better able to integrate these disadvantaged students into the academic environment. While counter to the initial hypothesis, it is possible that these schools may be able to better accommodate the needs of economically challenged students when the schools are centralized to a particular community. When parents, teachers, and school administrators know one another in the community, it is possible that the school and school activities become an extension of that community; resulting in a higher average bond found within the school.

Additional exploratory analysis of this finding suggests that the majority of the high poverty schools are located in one, rural county in the state. Thus, the majority of the poverty found in these high poverty schools is rural versus urban poverty. Further, the students in this particular county attend predominantly community-based schools. A cohort of students that begin elementary school together will in many cases attend the same middle and high school. At the middle school level, there are few options for these students outside of public school. Students can attend public school or be home schooled, since there are very few private schools in the area. With all of this taken into account, this finding may not be as counterintuitive as initially thought. This finding, however, may be unique to this particular state and thus not generalizable to the national public school population.

The results of this HLM analysis support the initial hypothesis suggesting that larger schools will experience a weaker average level of bonding. Larger schools are found to be more impersonal environments where students do not receive individual attention they need to feel comfortable and excel in their academic endeavors. When schools become too large, the school environment becomes less welcoming leaving little opportunity for prosocial bonding.

Schools that report an above average number of suspensions, expulsions, and zero tolerance expulsions handed out over the past academic year experience lower levels of school bonding. This supports the initial hypothesis, suggesting that schools with higher levels of discipline reduce the mean level of bonding found within a school. Previous research indicates that students feel targeted by school disciplinary measures. While it is feasible schools which maintain a level of control through the use of discipline measures may also make students feel safe and more bonded to the school; schools with high levels of discipline may also alienate students creating a hostile learning environment, weakening the average school bond within a school.

Finally, no support was found for the hypothesis suggesting the use of ability grouping would reduce the mean level of bonding in a school. While the effect of ability grouping was in the expected direction, the use of ability grouping does not significantly impact the mean level of bonding within a school. It is possible that in middle school, the stigma that is attached to lower academic tracks is not as salient among students. When ability grouping is less transparent to the students, the school bond is not significantly affected.

Further, no support was found for the hypothesis suggesting the average school bond will be lower in schools with higher levels of delinquency. The overall level of delinquency found within a school was not found to significantly impact the average bond between schools.

In addition, no support was found for the hypothesized interactions. The average level of delinquency in a school does not have a significant impact on the effect of gender on the school bond. Also, the effect of race on the school bond was not impacted by a school's minority enrollment. Further, school discipline was not found to significantly impact the effect of race on school bonding. Finally, the negative effect of delinquency on school bonding was not found to significantly differ between those schools that employ ability grouping and those which do not. However, two additional interaction effects were found to be significant.

The average effect of being male on the school bond was found to depend on the proportion of minorities enrolled in a school. When schools have a higher proportion of minorities enrolled, males within that school experience a slightly weaker bond to school than their female counterparts. As previously discussed the bussing situation for 8th grade students places white youth into a more diverse, urban environment. This finding may indicate that these White males are experiencing a weaker bond to school when placed in schools with larger minority populations.

The structure of a student's family, as well as the average age of students within a school were found to significantly affect the mean level of bonding within a school (Table 4.5; Two-parent home, Age). Students who reside with both parents experience a slightly higher, though statistically significant, level of school bonding than those who have other living arrangements. Thus, schools that have a higher number of students coming from intact families will see an increase in the mean level of school bonding within the school. However, schools with a high proportion of students above the mean class age, should experience lower levels of school bonding. These effects were not influenced by school variables.

Further academic achievement, as measured by average student GPA, was noted to have a significant differentiating effect on the school bond within schools (Table 4.5; GPA). More academically successful schools, at least successful in terms of reporting a higher overall grade point average (GPA), experience a higher average school bond. Only one between-school measure provided a significant change in the mean effect of grade point average on school bonding.

High proportions of punishment within a school reduced the positive effect of grade point average on school bonding within a school. While academically successful students might increase the overall school bond found in a school; harsh discipline measures within a school reduce this positive effect of GPA on the school bond. Thus the positive, average effect of GPA on school bonding is weakened by the negative affect of harsh discipline.

The reduction in the average effect of grade point average on school bonding between schools via school punishment is a finding worthy of note. It suggests that while academic success improves the average level of bonding in a school, harsh disciplinary action has a deleterious effect on this relationship.

It was also noted that the average effects of both delinquency and drug use reduce the average school bond across schools. This corresponds with the findings in the OLS models, and supports previous research finding a negative association between delinquency and the school bond. Also lending support to the initial hypotheses delinquency and drug use reduce an average student's bond to school. Also, since no contextual school variables were found to be significant, these findings suggest delinquency weakens the school bond regardless of the school environment.

The average effect of race, parent's education and delinquent peer associations on the school bond was not found to significantly vary across schools, indicating these factors do not have a differentiating effect on school bonding between schools. There was no support found for the hypothesis addressing the impact of school context variables on the racial gap in school bonding across schools.

Summary of 8th grade findings

School context was able to explain a larger proportion of the variation in school bonding than explained in the elementary school sample. Whereas one's bond to school in the 5th grade can be primarily explained through individual-level factors, the school context is able to enhance the explanation of the school bond for 8th grade students.

Support was found for the hypotheses that a higher grade point average and living with both parents, particularly those with high levels of education, help to increase a student's bond to school. Individual measures of age, delinquency, as well as association with delinquent peers significantly reduce the student-school bond, again supporting the initial hypotheses regarding the school bond. Race was found to have a significant effect on the school bond, but only among females. African American females experience a lower school bond than their male counterparts.

Significant differences were noted between gender and ethnic groups. It was determined that individual drug use and delinquent peer associations are more detrimental to the female school bond. In addition, African American males experience a stronger bond to school than their female counterparts. Additional differences were found between the White, African American and Non-African American minority samples. The effect of living with both parents on the school bond was significantly lower for Non-African American minorities as opposed to Whites and African Americans. Finally the effect of parent's level of education on the school bond was also found to be slightly lower for Non-African American minority students, though the interaction was not found to be statistically significant.

Support was also found for two school-level hypotheses. School enrollment and school punishment were found to significantly reduce the mean level of bonding found in a school. Contrary to the initial hypotheses, minority enrollment and proportion of students in poverty improved the mean school bond in a school. However, there was no support for the negative influence of ability grouping on the school bond in a school. There was also no support for the interaction hypotheses.

Table 4.5: Estimated Effects of School Context on School Bonding in the 8th Grade (School N= 31; Individual N=5018).[56,57]

Outcome	Parameter	Coefficient
Intercept		
Intercept	G00	4.50**
Ability Group	G01	-0.27
Enrollment	G02	-0.01*
Minority	G03	0.01*
Poverty	G04	0.01*
Punished	G05	-0.03*
Drug Use	G06	-0.17
Delinquency	G07	0.14
Male		
Intercept	G10	0.11
Ability Group	G11	-0.10
Enrollment	G12	-0.00
Minority	G13	-0.01*
Poverty	G14	0.00
Punished	G15	-0.00
Drug Use	G16	-0.05
Delinquency	G17	-0.06
African American		
Intercept	G20	-0.19
Ability Group	G21	-0.13
Enrollment	G22	0.00
Minority	G23	0.00
Poverty	G24	0.00
Punished	G25	0.00
Drug Use	G26	0.06
Delinquency	G27	-0.06
Non-African American Minority		
Intercept	G30	-0.14
Ability Group	G31	0.03
Enrollment	G32	0.00
Minority	G33	0.00
Poverty	G34	0.00
Punished	G35	0.00
Drug Use	G36	-0.03
Delinquency	G37	0.03

Table 4.5: Estimated Effects of School Context on School Bonding in the 8th Grade (School N= 31; Individual N=5018). (cont.)[56,57]

Outcome	Parameter	Coefficient
Lives with both parents		
Intercept	G40	0.01*
Ability Group	G41	0.03
Enrollment	G42	0.00
Minority	G43	0.00
Poverty	G44	-0.00
Punished	G45	0.00
Drug Use	G46	0.05
Delinquency	G47	-0.06
Age		
Intercept	G50	-0.08*
Ability Group	G51	0.00
Enrollment	G52	0.00
Minority	G53	0.00
Poverty	G54	-0.00
Punishment	G55	0.00
Drug Use	G56	0.00
Delinquency	G57	0.02
Grade Point Average		
Intercept	G60	0.10*
Ability Group	G61	0.05
Enrollment	G62	-0.00
Minority	G63	-0.00
Poverty	G64	-0.00
Punish	G65	-0.01**
Drug Use	G66	0.05
Delinquency	G67	-0.04
Parental Education Level		
Intercept	G70	0.00
Ability Group	G71	0.00
Enrollment	G72	0.00
Minority	G73	0.00
Poverty	G74	-0.00
Punish	G75	0.00
Drug Use	G76	-0.01
Delinquency	G77	-0.01

Table 4.5: Estimated Effects of School Context on School Bonding in the 8th Grade (School N= 31; Individual N=5018). (cont.)[56,57]

Outcome	Parameter	Coefficient
Drug Use		
Intercept	G80	-0.02*
Ability Group	G81	0.01
Enrollment	G82	0.00
Minority	G83	0.00
Poverty	G84	0.00
Punish	G85	-0.00
Drug Use	G86	0.00
Delinquency	G87	-0.00
Delinquency		
Intercept	G90	-0.04**
Ability Group	G91	-0.01
Enrollment	G92	0.00
Minority	G93	0.00
Poverty	G94	-0.00
Punish	G95	-0.00
Drug Use	G96	-0.00
Delinquency	G97	-0.00
Association with Delinquent Peers		
Intercept	G100	-0.00
Ability Group	G101	-0.00
Enrollment	G102	-0.00
Minority	G103	0.00
Poverty	G104	-0.00
Punished	G105	-0.00
Drug Use	G106	-0.00
Delinquency	G107	0.01

Chapter 5

The High School Bonding Experience

The high school experience is often a memorable, yet harrowing one for students. Many people look back fondly on their high school years but would never want to relive that time of their lives. It is during the high school years that adolescents continue their quest for independence, gain a better understanding of themselves as individuals, and set goals for the future. Rarely is this an easy journey. However, by the time a student reaches 11th grade much of his or her development has occurred.

By the late high school years, most students have gained an increased level of independence marked by increased autonomy, greater emotional stability, and the ability to weigh the promises and perils of a decision. Conflicts with parents have declined, and a student has a more cohesive sense of his or her own identity as well as a better developed ability for compromise. Peer associations remain of the utmost importance, ranking as some of the most salient relationships in the young person's life to this point.

During the late high school years, particularly around the 11th grade, students begin to place an importance on their future. Their work habits become more defined and students begin setting goals for the coming years. Students also increasingly recognize their own self-esteem, taking pride in their work and future aspirations. It is also important to note here, that by the time students reach the 11th grade they are free to leave the public school system, in effect ending their education. Therefore, those students who did not place a high value on a high school education will not be present in the following analyses.

The following analyses explore the impact of individual characteristics and the school context on the school bond among high school students. Again, individual characteristics such as race, gender, family structure, parental education, and participation in delinquency were studied to assess the individual-level impact on the student-school bond relationship. Further, contextual variables of a school such as school size, minority enrollment, proportion of students in poverty, discipline measures, and the use of ability grouping were employed to assess the between school differences found to impact the student-school bond at the high school level.

This chapter will provide a description of the 11th grade sample, followed by an analysis of both the individual- and school-level variables.

Sample Descriptives
Table 5.1 presents the means and standard deviations for the 11th grade sample. The 11th grade sample included 3,901 students. Roughly 50 percent of the sample was male, 22 percent reported their race as African American, and roughly 11 percent defined themselves as Non-African American minority. The mean age of the sample was 16.6; indicating the average 11th grade student in the population was almost 17 years old at the time the data were collected. In addition, 56 percent of the students in the 11th grade sample resided with both parents.

The descriptives for the school context variables indicate just over half of the schools employ ability grouping. That is to say that about half of the public schools within the state report classifying students based on perceived ability in Math and English courses. The average enrollment across the high schools in the sample was 1,243 students, with an average minority enrollment of 36 percent and an average of 23 percent of students enrolled in the free and reduced lunch program.

11th Grade Individual Level Effects
Table 5.2 presents an OLS regression model for all students in the 11th grade sample followed by the regression model split by gender and then by race. The regression model examined the effect of the demographic variables, family structure, individual grade point average, mean level of parental education and delinquency variables on the individual's bond to school.

These demographic, family and delinquency variables were able to explain 25 percent of the variation in school bonding for 11th grade students. Eight of the ten variables were found to be significant predictors: age, gender, family structure, parents education, GPA, delinquency, drug use and association with delinquent peers.

Table 5.1: Descriptive Statistics for 11th grade Public School and School Students in a Mid Atlantic State.[58]

Variable	Mean	St.Dev.	Minimum	Maximum
Individual-Level				
School Bond	26.22	6.19	7.00	41.00
Age	16.60	0.64	13.00	16.00
Sex	0.49	0.50	0.00	1.00
African American	0.22	0.41	0.00	1.00
Non-African American Minority	0.11	0.32	0.00	1.00
Grade Point Average	2.84	0.84	1.00	4.00
Lives with both Parents	0.55	0.50	0.00	1.00
Parent's Education	13.00	3.86	0.00	18.00
Drug Use	17.06	5.75	1.00	87.00
Delinquency	13.75	5.18	8.00	48.00
Association With Delinquent Peers	16.51	5.82	7.00	35.00

Table 5.1: Descriptive Statistics for 11th grade Public School and School Students in a Mid Atlantic State (cont.).[58]

Variable	Mean	St.Dev.	Minimum	Maximum
School-Level				
School Enrollment	1242.74	397.28	472.00	2196.00
Ability Grouping	0.51	0.50	0.00	1.00
Free and Reduced Lunch	22.63	5.28	6.38	34.89
Minority Enrollment	35.89	10.90	13.22	57.64
Use of Punishment	25.64	16.46	2.69	77.28
School Drug Use	17.05	0.70	15.79	19.28
School Delinquency	13.73	0.66	12.15	15.60

The strongest predictor of school bonding among 11th grade students is grade point average (beta= 0.27). Students with higher GPA's, indicating level of academic achievement, exhibit higher levels of school bonding. By the time a student reaches the 11th grade, he or she is already looking toward the future. Those students who plan to continue their education must have good grades, but also be well-rounded individuals. Those students who are pursuing vocational careers may also be experiencing the same success in vocational programs, reaffirming a desire for the chosen career path. Thus, a student who is achieving academic success will exhibit stronger bonds to school.

Parents' educational attainment was also found to be a significant predictor of a student's school bond. Intuitively, parental education should be one of the strongest correlates of a student's academic achievement. Parents who place an emphasis on the importance of education will encourage their child to succeed and continue on to college. When college is a known entity to parents, they can support and assist their child in gaining a college education.

At a more basic level, however, the average level of parent's education should indicate the value placed on education in the home setting. When education is valued and accentuated as a positive experience, it is likely that a student will mirror the sentiments of his or her parent(s). Further, and as discussed in the previous chapter, better educated parents provide their children with social and cultural capital to assure a successful school experience. Again, these parents usually have the means, but also understand the value of encyclopedias, computers, and periodical subscriptions in the home. This finding supports the initial hypothesis suggesting the higher the level of education achieved by the parent the greater the level of school bonding experienced by the student.

Parents have an additional impact on the bond a student has with the school. Students who reside with both parents also experience a greater level of school bonding. Again, the value placed on education within the home is a significant part of the experience for a child. Living with both parents, it is likely that a child would receive a uniform message about the importance of education as well as support for his or her academic endeavors. Moreover, when a child comes from a one-parent home, that parent is the only one available to get involved with the student's activities and academics.

In many cases, a one parent home requires that parent to work in order to sustain a livable wage. A single parent has little or no support when his or her child gets sick and has to leave school, has a school play during work hours, or gets in trouble and is expelled from school. There is less time for the parent to spend involved in parent/teacher associations, at school related functions, or simply getting to know his or her child's own teachers.

A two parent home can split the child-rearing responsibilities. One parent can drive the student to school and the other pick him or her up from school if they do not already drive or take the bus. The two parent household is more likely to manage the time demands of taking their child to and from 'practices' or help their child purchase a car if he or she is over 16. In addition, if a family has more than one child, the two parent household is able to support multiple children, and their activities, by splitting up the responsibilities; One parent can go to one sporting event while the other is at another. Theoretically, there is simply twice the person-power it takes to raise a child, be present in that child's life, and support his or her activities and academic successes.

Males were found to have a lower level of school bonding than females. While these students are towards the end of their adolescent development, they are still experiencing conflict. Boys continue to push the levels of acceptable behavior within the school setting. Even with a more developed sense of self-esteem boys will fight back when their masculinity is challenged, which is a relatively common behavior in the high school setting. While the rash of school shootings that occurred during the late 1990's into early 2000 are statistically rare incidences, the bullying and ostracizing that preceded these incidences are not so rare, particularly among high school males.

Age is also a significant predictor of the individual's bond to school. As noted in the 8th grade population and in support of the initial hypothesis, the older students in a class are likely to feel less bonded to the school.

An older student in an 11th grade classroom would place someone between 17 and 19 years old. Around this age, kids are able to drive, hold a part time job, vote, and enlist in the armed services. The freedom of having a driver's license and disposable income from a part time job may pull a teen away from school work towards the lure of fun and excitement. If these students are working part time during the school year, they have less time available for school activities and homework. Spending less time involved with school would lead to a significant reduction in the student-school bond. In addition, older students in the 11th grade are likely to have been held back a year in school, and are developmentally out of sync with their peers.

Again contrary to the initial hypothesis, the effect of being African American or Non-African American minority does not significantly impact a student's bond to school. This is a surprising finding given the body of research indicating the disconnectedness experienced by African Americans in the American educational system. However, an additional analysis will be conducted to assess the significant differences in the effect of these variables on race/ethnicity and gender specific models.

In support of the initial research hypotheses, the regression results also indicate individual substance use, delinquency and association with delinquent peers each significantly reduced the bond to school.

When students are using drugs or alcohol, the effects of these substances can impact school performance. A student who comes to school high or with a hangover is less likely to be able to concentrate and work at peak performance. When students use drugs which dull or numb their senses, there is no way they can perform as well as they would without the substance.

Further, the culture of drug use among high school students is usually characterized by a disregard for academic achievement. While some students may attempt to 'kill the pain' of stress by abusing stimulants or prescription pain killers, most use alcohol, marijuana or other illicit substance as an escape from the stressors of reality. The desire to escape from reality indicates a separation from the school culture which would theoretically lead to a reduction of the school bond.

There are also consequences to one's reputation when labeled into a delinquent subculture. If a student is labeled a 'druggie' students and school personnel who disapprove of this behavior are more likely to treat the student differently. This labeling may lead to a disassociation with school again weakening the school bond.

Participation in delinquent activities also significantly reduces the student-school bond, again supporting the initial hypothesis. Those students who are involved with more delinquent activities, such as fighting, stealing and trespassing may engage in more frequent delinquent behavior again precluding them from spending a sufficient amount of time on school work or in school related activities to exhibit a strong bond to school. But again, delinquent behavior can impact interaction at school. Students and teachers alike know the students are participating in delinquency, and in many cases are likely to avoid them for fear of being labeled as a delinquent themselves. In addition, many students fear those who are the 'bully' or 'aggressive' or even 'druggies'. Participation in this behavior, and the isolation that comes with it, is likely to lead to a disconnect from school thus weakening the school bond.

Finally, and in support of the initial hypothesis, association with delinquent peers was found to significantly reduce the bond to school. Association with a peer group is an important part of the high school experience. Therefore the group with which one associates is likely to influence behavior.

By the time students enter high school their peer group is a reflection of their own views. Students seek peers with values that are similar to their own, even if these values are counter to those taught in the school. When one associates with delinquent peers, it is likely that the values of this group promote delinquency rather than school connectedness. In order to fit into this peer group, a student is likely to adopt the values of his or her peers if he or she does not already share them.

Students may also experience negative consequences to their reputation when associating with delinquent peers. As noted with delinquency and drug use, students may experience alienation from the larger student body or school personnel when associating with delinquent peers. Every student in the school is well aware of each other's social status and the status of those with whom they associate. Thus, for fear of being associated with the 'bad kids' and the stigma that will place on their own reputation, students may pull away from individuals who are associated with a delinquent peer group further isolating the delinquents from the larger school community. Thus association with delinquent peers has been found to significantly reduce a students bond to school.

Table 5.2: Regression Coefficients Predicting School Bonding Among 11th Grade Public School Students.[59]

Variable	All 11th	Coefficient (beta) 11th Gender		11th Race		
		Male	Female	White	African American	Non-African American Minority
Constant	32.81	28.27	34.40	31.26	33.66	4.87
Male	-0.89*** (-0.07)			-1.32***	0.16	-0.67
African American	0.17 (0.01)	1.03**	-0.63*			
Non-African American Minority	-0.27 (-0.01)	-0.05	-0.45			
Age	-0.62*** (-0.07)	-0.44*	-0.84***	-0.58***	-0.58*	-0.96**
Living with Both Parents	0.96*** (0.08)	0.73**	1.19***	1.01***	0.83*	0.57
Grade Point Average	1.99*** (0.27)	1.99***	1.95***	2.13***	1.58***	1.52***
Parent's Education	0.23*** (0.14)	0.24***	0.21***	0.29***	0.09*	0.29***
Drug Use	-0.05** (-0.05)	-0.03	-0.08**	-0.02	-0.09	-0.10
Delinquency	-0.05* (-0.05)	-0.01	-0.14***	-0.05	-0.01	-0.14*
Association with Delinquent Peers	-0.20*** (-0.19)	-0.24***	-0.15***	-0.25***	-0.14***	-0.11*
Adjusted R-Square	0.25	0.22	0.24	0.30	0.12	0.24
N	3937	2048	1889	2643	837	456

Gender Differences in 11th Grade School Bonding

Noting that males exhibited significantly lower levels of school bonding, an additional analysis was conducted to test the equivalency of models between the sexes. These results can also be found in Table 5.2. This analysis attempts to flesh out differences in the effects of individual level variables between males and females. The results of the Chow test indicate that there is a significant difference in the male and female models in the 11th grade population ($F=435.90$; $p> 0.001$).

The gender specific models, like the full regression model, examined the effect of the demographic control variables, the family variables, grade point average, and delinquency variables on the school bond.

Twenty-two percent of the variation in male school bonds and 24 percent of the variation in female school bonds can be explained by this set of variables.

Students with higher grade point averages, whether they are male or female, were found to exhibit higher levels of school bonding. Further, those students coming from a household with well-educated parents also exhibited higher levels of school bonding regardless of sex. Age was found to reduce school bonds for both males and females. In addition, students experience higher levels of school bonding when they live with both parents. Again, this finding was noted for both genders.

While race was found to be a significant predictor of school bonding for both 11th grade males and females, being African American improve the male's bond to school while reducing the female's bond. African American males experience a higher level of school bonding than White and Non-African American minorities. This follows in line with the results from the 8th grade male-only models.

Individual drug use was found to diminish a female's bond to school, but did not quite reach significance for males. Again, previous research has indicated the negative effect drug use has on individual academic achievement. Particularly at the high school level, it is interesting to note that the influence of drug use on the student-school bond relationship continues to differ based on gender as was noted in the earlier grades. Further, participation in delinquent behavior also diminishes a student's bond to school. This is again true for females, while not reaching significance for males. Delinquent peer associations; however, diminish a student's school bond, regardless of gender. That is to say that if a male or female associates with a delinquent peer group, they will report a lower level of attachment to, commitment to, and involvement in school.

Noting the differences in the effect of individual variables on the school bond for males and females, five interaction terms were created and added to the model to test if the effect of being African American, individual drug use and individual delinquency on the school bond are significantly different between the sexes.

Table 5.3 presents the results of this analysis. Model 2 indicates that the effect of being African American is significantly different for males and females. Being African American significantly improves males' bond to school, however, the same cannot be said for females.

Model 3 indicates that the effect of age does not significantly differ between males and females. Model 4 presents the results of a test for significant differences in the effect of residing with both parents on school bonding. The positive effect of residing with both parents is significantly less for males than females. Finally, Models 5 and 6 present the results of a test for significant differences in the effects of individual drug use and delinquency on school bonding between the genders. It was noted that both drug use and delinquency are more detrimental to the female's bond to school than the male's bond.

In summary, when a female is delinquent or uses drugs, her bond to school is affected. The positive impact of living with both parents was noted to be weaker for males than females. However, the effect of being African American significantly improved a male's bond to school while having a significant, negative effect on the female school bond.

Racial Differences in School Bonding for 11th grade students
The results of the regression models separated by race/ethnic category are the last three models in Table 5.2. Table 5.4 presents the effects of race interactions to assess significant differences in the effects of individual variables across the race/ethnic categories. Chow Tests indicate that the White, African American, and Non-African American minority models are not equivalent to one another.[61]

The race/ethnic specific models, like the full regression model, examined the effect of the demographic control variables, the family variables, grade point average, and delinquency variables on the school bond. This model was able to explain 30 percent of the variation in the White-only school bond, 12 percent of the variation in African American school bonds and 24 percent of the variation in Non-African American minority school bonds.

The OLS results indicated that the effect of being male only significantly reduces White's bond to school. The effect of being male, while in the expected direction given the gender specific results, is not statistically significant for the African American sample. This finding conflicts with the results of the gender specific models which suggest that African American males experience a stronger bond to school than White males. While the finding that the White males experience lower bonds is in line with the gender specific finding that African American males experience a stronger bond to school than White males, there would still be an expectation that the effect of being male would be significant in the African American-only model.

Table 5.3: Regression Coefficients Predicting School Bonding Among 11th Grade Public School Students With Gender Interaction (N=3901).[60]

Variable	Model 1	Model 2	Coefficient (beta) Model 3	Model 4	Model 5	Model 6
Constant	32.81	32.90	36.77	32.67	33.25	33.78
Male	-0.89*** (-0.07)	-1.24*** (-0.07)	-0.86* (-0.07)	-0.46 (-0.04)	-1.58*** (-0.13)	-2.09*** (-0.17)
African American	0.17 (0.01)	-0.66* (0.04)	0.18 (0.01)	0.16 (0.01)	0.17 (0.01)	0.16 (0.01)
Non-African American Minority	-0.27 (-0.01)	-0.27 (-0.01)	-0.28 (-0.01)	-0.25 (-0.01)	-0.27 (-0.01)	-0.28 (-0.01)
Age	-0.62*** (-0.07)	-0.62*** (-0.06)	-0.86*** (-0.09)	-0.63*** (-0.07)	-0.63*** (-0.07)	-0.64*** (-0.07)
Living with Both Parents	0.96*** (0.08)	0.98*** (0.08)	0.96*** (0.08)	1.33*** (0.10)	0.95*** (0.08)	0.94*** (0.08)
Grade Point Average	1.99*** (0.27)	1.98*** (0.27)	1.99*** (0.27)	1.99*** (0.27)	1.99*** (0.27)	1.98*** (0.27)
Parents Education	0.23*** (0.14)	0.23*** (0.14)	0.23*** (0.14)	0.23*** (0.14)	0.23*** (0.14)	0.23*** (0.14)
Drug Use	-0.05** (-0.05)	-0.05** (-0.05)	-0.05* (-0.05)	-0.05** (-0.05)	-0.07** (-0.07)	-0.05** (-0.05)

Delinquency	-0.05* (-0.05)	-0.06* (-0.05)	-0.20*** (-0.19)	-0.05* (-0.05)	-0.06** (-0.05)	-0.12*** (-0.10)
Association with Delinquent Peers	-0.20*** (-0.19)	-0.20*** (-0.19)		-0.20*** (-0.19)	-0.20*** (-0.19)	-0.20*** (-0.19)
Male* African American		1.72** (0.08)	0.47 (0.03)			
Male * Age						
Male * Family				-0.76* (-0.06)		
Male* Drugs					0.04* (0.06)	
Male* Delinquency			0.25			0.09* (0.12)
Adjusted R-Square	0.25	0.25		0.25	0.25	0.25

Table 5.4: Regression Coefficients Predicting School Bonding Among 11th Grade Public School Students with Race Interaction (N=3091). [62]

Variable	Model 1	Model 2	Model 3	Model 4	Model 5	Model 6	Model 7	Model 8
Constant	32.81	33.37	32.38	32.81	32.26	31.81	32.71	32.85
Male	-0.89*** (-0.07)	-0.34* (-0.04)	-0.88*** (-0.07)	-0.89*** (-0.07)	-0.87*** (-0.07)	-0.90*** (-0.07)	-0.88*** (-0.07)	-0.89*** (-0.07)
African American	0.17 (0.01)	0.34 (0.01)	0.17 (0.01)	0.17 (0.01)	0.17 (0.01)	2.89* (0.19)	0.17 (0.01)	0.07 (0.01)
Non-African American Minority	-0.27 (-0.01)	-0.57 (-0.03)	0.18 (0.06)	-0.27 (-0.01)	-0.14 (-0.01)	-0.25 (-0.01)	-0.40 (-0.02)	-0.37 (-0.02)
Age	-0.62*** (-0.07)	-0.62*** (-0.07)	-0.60*** (-0.06)	-0.62*** (-0.07)	-0.61*** (-0.06)	-0.61*** (-0.06)	-0.62*** (-0.07)	-0.63*** (-0.07)
Living with Both Parents	0.96*** (0.08)	0.99*** (0.08)	0.96*** (0.08)	0.96*** (0.08)	0.94*** (0.08)	0.93*** (0.07)	0.96*** (0.08)	0.96*** (0.08)
Grade Point Average	1.99*** (0.27)	1.95*** (0.26)	1.99*** (0.27)	1.99*** (0.27)	1.57*** (0.21)	1.96*** (0.27)	1.99*** (0.27)	1.99*** (0.27)
Parent's Education	0.23*** (0.14)	0.22*** (0.13)	0.23*** (0.14)	0.23*** (0.14)	0.22*** (0.14)	0.29*** (0.18)	0.23*** (0.14)	0.23*** (0.14)
Drug Use	-0.05** (-0.05)	-0.05* (-0.04)	-0.05** (-0.05)	-0.05** (-0.05)	-0.05** (-0.05)	-0.05* (-0.05)	-0.05** (-0.05)	-0.05* (-0.05)
Delinquency	-0.05* (-0.05)	-0.05* (-0.04)	-0.05* (-0.05)	-0.05* (-0.05)	-0.05* (-0.05)	-0.05* (-0.05)	-0.05* (-0.05)	-0.05* (-0.05)

Association with Delinquent Peers	-0.20*** (-0.19)	-0.20*** (-0.20)	-0.20*** (-0.19)	-0.20*** (-0.19)	-0.20*** (-0.19)	-0.20*** (-0.19)	-0.20*** (-0.19)	-0.20*** (-0.19)
White * Male		-1.41*** (0.11)						
Non-African American Minority * Age			-0.21 (-0.17)					
Non-African American Minority * Parents				0.03 (0.00)				
White* GPA					0.61*** (0.15)			
African American * Parents Education						-0.22*** (-0.19)		
Non-African American Minority * Delinquency							-0.05 (-0.04)	
White* Delinquent Peers								- 0.01 (0.01)
Adjusted R-Square	0.25	0.25	0.25	0.25	0.25	0.25	0.25	0.25

One reason for this inconsistent finding may could be due to sample size. The male-only sample is roughly two and a half times larger (N=1964) than the African American-only sample (N=837). Though the male-only sample is not remarkably large, it is substantial enough that an effect size of 1.03 in that sample would figure to be significant. The significant difference in the effect of being male will be tested further in additional analysis presented in Table 5.4. These findings will be discussed shortly.

Grade point average was found to significantly improve a student's bond to school regardless of a student's race. Students coming from homes where their parents are more highly educated also experience a stronger school bond regardless of race/ethnic background.

Family structure also influences a student's bond to school. Those students who reside in a two-parent home are found to have a significantly higher level of school bonding than those who do not reside with both parents. This was found to be the case for White and African American students, but does not reach significance for Non-African American minorities.

Culturally Hispanic populations, the predominant majority of the Non-African American population, place a strong emphasis on family, so it is interesting to note that family structure has no significant impact on the bond to school. However, it may not be as unexpected as initially thought. The Hispanic population is one of the few populations that continue to emphasize the importance of extended family. With a cultural importance placed on parents, grandparents, and other familial ties, it may not really matter who a student actually lives with in the home. Family may be an important influence on a student's attachment to school, not necessarily who resides within a student's home.

Age was found to decrease a student's bond to school for African American, White, and Non-African American minority students. Regardless of race, older students experience weaker bonds to school.

Drug use was not found to have a significant effect on the school bond for the race/ethnic categories individually. However, individual delinquency and delinquent peer associations were found to negatively impact the school bond for Non-African American minorities. The effect of delinquent peer associations was found to reduce the bond for Whites and African Americans as well as Non-African American minorities.

Table 5.4 presents the results of additional regression models run to test for significant differences in the effects noted in the race/ethnic specific models between groups. Three interaction terms were found to be significant. The effect of being male on the school bond is found to be most detrimental for Whites. However, the positive effect of grade point average on the school bond is found to be stronger for White students. Finally, the positive effect of parental education is not quite as strong for African Americans. That is, an African American student's school bond is not as strongly influenced by the education of his or her parents.

School-Level Effects for the 11th Grade

Table 5.5 presents the effects of school context variables on school bonding in the 11th grade. The variance in the intercept in the conditional model was found to be significant (τ=0.02; df=29; χ^2 = 43.34; p=0.03) and also below the unconditional model suggesting additional variation in the mean level of school bonding is explained by individual level predictors. Approximately 8 percent of the variation in the mean level of school bonding can be explained by the between school measures. Only two school contextual variables were found to have a significant effect on the mean level of bonding found within a school. This analysis indicates a school's use of ability grouping and the proportion of students receiving free and reduced lunch within a school made a significant impact on the mean level of school bonding found in the schools.

The mean level of school bonding found in schools that employ ability grouping is significantly lower than in those schools that do not use ability grouping, supporting the initial hypothesis. High schools that employ ability grouping are those with a mix of students; some who are college bound others who are not. Those schools which do not employ ability grouping most likely have more uniform student populations, such as a vocational school or a college preparatory school. While there are no private schools in this sample, there are certain public high schools within this state which send a majority of their students to college. It is possible that those schools, whose students are all predominantly focused on similar goals, whether it is a vocational career or college, may be able to better service the students. Schools that manage a college preparatory curriculum, intermediate curriculum, and remedial curriculum may be less able to integrate all students, leaving some more isolated than others. The use of ability grouping in the school was expected to negatively impact the student-school bond since schools which mix college bound students and non-academic track students are bound to have students who are unintentionally marginalized.

It is interesting to note that ability grouping has only been found to have a significant impact on the 11th grade school bond, not for the 5th or 8th grade, indicating the use of ability grouping in high school context is more detrimental to the student's bond to school than ever before.

A rather interesting finding was that the proportion of poverty in a school significantly improves the average bond found in a school. This positive effect was also noted in the 8th grade sample, though it continues to be contrary to the initial hypothesis. One thought on this finding comes from recognizing the legal age at which students can drop out of school in the state. Students are free to cease ties with the public school system in the 10th grade. Those students who choose not to return for their junior and senior years are free to do so. So, this sample of 11th grade students has already seen the first wave of drops out exit the sample. By the time that student reaches the 11th grade, those students who are in poverty have made the conscious decision to stay in the school; thus showing an affinity for and commitment to the school itself. The descriptive statistics reflect a reduction in the percent of students receiving free or reduced lunch in the 11th grade, suggesting that there are fewer low income students in the 11th grade as opposed to earlier grades.

While the measure of poverty is a proportion for the school, this finding could be an artifact of an untapped indicator of school bonding which is future aspiration, also explaining the significant finding in the 8th grade sample. This finding could indicate a cultural value of education or understanding the need for at least a high school education which is one component of the school bond. The higher the proportion of students in poverty at a school may actually indicate a commitment to school among the group who are at a high risk of dropping out. So, while contrary to the initial hypothesis, this finding may not be that counterintuitive. If the proportion of students in poverty remains above average in a school, it may actually indicate a level of commitment and affinity for school rather than a risk factor as noted in previous research. Of course, it must be noted that this effect was found to be significant while controlling for many of the negative correlates of poverty.

However, schools that are based in a community where poverty is known may also be better suited to integrate low-income students into the academic environment. If, for instance, the school is based in a rural area and the center of a community, the school administration may be aware of the needs of the community and attempt to cater to these needs. Schools in these rural areas may provide professional skills training, such as computer programming or vocational alternatives to a college preparatory curriculum. In other words, these schools may have developed tactics to avoid marginalizing a population in poverty, unlike other schools where poverty is less common. Schools which are successful at integrating students from different social backgrounds, such as low-income students, should experience a higher average bond to school.

Other between-school measures had little impact on the mean level of bonding found in schools. Indicators such as school size, proportion of minorities enrolled within a school, level of delinquency and drug use in a school, and in particular the use of discipline yielded no significant between-school differences in the mean level of school bonding at the high school level, providing no support for the initial hypotheses. Further these school-level indicators were not found to have a moderating impact on the effect of other individual-level variables on the school bond for students within a given school.

The 11th grade findings reveal that schools which employ ability grouping have a lower level of school bonding than those schools which do not employ ability grouping. Unlike the in the 5th and 8th grade, variables such as size and minority enrollment have no significant between-schools impact on the level of school bonding.

While proportion of students on free and reduced lunch had no effect on school bonding in the 5th grade, it was found to significantly improve the mean level of bonding in the 11th grade schools. Controlling for other variables, those schools with an above average proportion of students receiving the free and reduced lunch program on average experienced a higher level of bonding within their school than those schools with an average or below average proportion of students in poverty.

Additional between-schools variables such as amount of delinquency and drug use found in a school were also found to be insignificant factors on the mean level of bonding found in a school. While this is a non-finding, it is important to mention particularly under the scrutiny of current education policies focusing on 'dangerous' or 'violent' schools. While additional research is needed to study these issues, the negative effect of drug use, delinquency and delinquent peer associations on the school bond was not impacted by the school context. There was no support found for previous research indicating that larger schools diminish school attachment or connectedness.

Summary of 11th Grade Analysis of School Bonding

As true in the previous grades, the school bond at the high school level continues to primarily be an individual phenomenon. While the high school context was able to explain the largest proportion of variation in the average level of bonding found in any of the three grades, the majority of the variation remains explained by the individual level predictors. Thus, future research focusing on the student-school bond should continue to concentrate on those individual characteristics that predict a student's attachment to, commitment to, involvement at, and hopefully belief in his or her school.

This research indicates factors such as gender, age, family structure, grade point average, parental education, individual drug use, delinquency, and association with delinquent peers significantly influence a high school students bond to school. Not surprisingly, grade point average is the strongest predictor of a strong bond to school. Further, if the school context is of interest, factors such as the use of ability grouping and proportion of students in poverty provide an important starting point for future research on the high school bond.

Table 5.5: Estimated Effects of The School Environment on School Bonding in the 11th Grade.[63,64]

Outcome	Parameter	Coefficient
Intercept		
Intercept	G00	2.75
Ability Group	G01	-0.79***
Enrollment	G02	0.00
Minority	G03	-0.01
Poverty	G04	0.11**
Punished	G05	-0.05
Drug Use	G06	-0.05
Delinquency	G07	-0.57
Male		
Intercept	G10	0.12
Ability Group	G11	-0.25
Enrollment	G12	-0.00
Minority	G13	0.00
Poverty	G14	0.00
Punished	G15	-0.03
Drug Use	G16	-0.06
Delinquency	G17	-0.07
African American		
Intercept	G20	0.23
Ability Group	G21	-0.01
Enrollment	G22	-0.00
Minority	G23	0.00
Poverty	G24	0.01
Punished	G25	0.00
Drug Use	G26	-0.08
Delinquency	G27	-0.02
Non-African American Minority		
Intercept	G30	-0.07
Ability Group	G31	0.02
Enrollment	G32	0.00
Minority	G33	0.01
Poverty	G34	0.02
Punished	G35	-0.00
Drug Use	G36	-0.10
Delinquency	G37	0.08

Table 5.5: Estimated Effects of The School Environment on School Bonding in the 11th Grade (cont.).[63,64]

Outcome	Parameter	Coefficient
Lives with Both Parents		
Intercept	G40	0.00
Ability Group	G41	-0.03
Enrollment	G42	0.00
Minority	G43	-0.00
Poverty	G44	-0.00
Punished	G45	0.01
Drug Use	G46	0.02
Delinquency	G47	-0.03
Age		
Intercept	G50	-0.03
Ability Group	G51	0.05
Enrollment	G52	-0.00
Minority	G53	0.00
Poverty	G54	0.00
Punishment	G55	0.00
Drug Use	G56	0.00
Delinquency	G57	0.04
Grade Point Average		
Intercept	G60	0.33
Ability Group	G61	-0.06
Enrollment	G62	-0.00
Minority	G63	-0.01
Poverty	G64	0.01
Punishment	G65	-0.00
Drug Use	G66	0.01
Delinquency	G67	-0.02
Parental Education Level		
Intercept	G70	0.01
Ability Group	G71	0.00
Enrollment	G72	0.00
Minority	G73	-0.00
Poverty	G74	-0.00
Punished	G75	0.00
Drug Use	G76	0.00
Delinquency	G77	0.00

Table 5.5: Estimated Effects of The School Environment on School Bonding in the 11th Grade (cont.).[63,64]

Outcome	Parameter	Coefficient
Drug Use		
Intercept	G80	-0.00
Ability Group	G81	-0.00
Enrollment	G82	0.00
Minority	G83	-0.00
Poverty	G84	-0.00
Punished	G85	-0.00
Drug Use	G86	-0.00
Delinquency	G87	-0.00
Delinquency		
Intercept	G90	-0.02
Ability Group	G91	0.00
Enrollment	G92	0.00
Minority	G93	0.00
Poverty	G94	0.00
Punished	G95	0.00
Drug Use	G96	0.00
Delinquency	G97	0.00
Association with Delinquent Peers		
Intercept	G100	-0.01
Ability Group	G101	0.00
Enrollment	G102	-0.00
Minority	G103	-0.00
Poverty	G104	-0.00
Punished	G105	-0.00
Drug Use	G106	0.00
Delinquency	G107	0.00

Chapter 6

Conclusions and Policy Implications

This study focused on the student-school bond and what individual characteristics along with the school contextual factors influence that relationship. Most previous research addresses the school bond as a protective factor in a study of individual delinquency; however, few sociological studies have addressed the development of the school bond. This study was unique in that it focused on the examination of the school bond in three populations; 5th, 8th, and 11th grade students, being one of the first of its kind to address the issue of school bonding at the elementary school level. The student-school bond relationship was studied at both the individual level and school level to determine what factors affect the school bond and how these findings could assist in shaping social policy.

This study adds to the current literature by addressing the factors which impact the development of one's bond to school, and including the school-level variables and between-school effects on the study of the school bond. Again, employing both sociological and developmental explanations for the findings, this research was able to follow the effect of school contextual variables between the elementary, middle, and high school levels.

Support for Research Hypotheses

Support was found for a number of the initial research hypotheses. By the time students reached the 8th grade, the effect of being male was found to reduce the school bond. Previous research indicates that males have a more difficult time negotiating school. Gilligan (1991) noted females are more likely to develop attachments to teachers, principals, and school administrators because they are able to 'do school' more so than males. In 'doing school', girls remain invisible to adults in the school environment by acting in a traditionally appropriate manner.

This finding supports previous research suggesting males experience a weaker bond to school than females.

Previous research also indicated older students in a classroom experience higher levels of disconnectedness and alienation from school (see Bonny, et. al., 2000; McNeal, 1995). This study supported the previous assertions, finding age to significantly reduce the bond to school for middle and high school students.

Residing with both parents was found to significantly improve a student's bond to school. While previous research has not directly addressed the impact of family structure on the school bond this finding, coupled with previous findings that note two-parent families are more likely to be involved in a child's education and school activities, suggest children from two-parent families experience a stronger bond to school.

Further, parent's educational attainment was found to significantly influence the school bond. Previous studies have noted that parents with a higher level of education are better able to help their children navigate the educational experience (see Paulson, 1994; Steinberg, 1993; West, 1982). Not only are these better educated parents more likely to provide educational resources to their children, but they may also discuss the importance of education and post-secondary schooling; all of which is found to improve a student's regard for school.

An ample body of research indicates academic performance is associated with school bonds (see: Maddox & Prinz, 2003; Lopez, Ehly, & Garcia-Vazquez, 2002). This study also indicates that in 8th and 11th grade, students with higher GPA's report stronger bonds to school.

Drug use, delinquency, and association with delinquent peers were each found to significantly reduce the school bond. While there is a substantial body of research indicating that a strong bond to school reduces drug use (see: Maddox & Prinz, 2003; Hawkins, et. al., 1997; Catalano, et. al., 1996), delinquency (see: Simons-Morton, et. al., 1999; Jenkins, 1995; Cernkovich & Giordano, 1992) and association with delinquent peers (see: Warr & Stafford, 1991; Matsueda & Heimer, 1987; Elliott, et. al., 1985), these findings support the assertion that the directionality of these relationships can in fact go both ways. That is, a strong bond to school may reduce individual delinquency; however, participation in delinquency will also reduce a student's bond to school.

This research contended that in order to look at the student-school bond, contextual variables such as the use of ability grouping, school enrollment, proportion of minorities enrolled, proportion of students in poverty, proportion of students who are disciplined in the school, and the level of delinquency and drug use within each school must be examined to provide a larger picture than individual differences in predicting the school bond. While the contextual variables did not explain a large proportion of difference between schools, the models did provide support for the initial hypotheses.

Larger middle schools were found to experience a lower mean level of school bonding.[65] Jackson Toby (1993) found that smaller schools have a stronger sense of community, in part, because of greater individualized attention by teachers. Further, Ascher (1994) suggests that students feel unsafe in larger schools which impact their ability to develop personal relationships with faculty and administrators. While this finding is unique to the middle school sample, it suggests that this age group is at greater risk for feeling unsafe or ostracized from the school environment. While many policy makers are focusing attention on school safety and connectedness at the high school level, this finding suggests that the same focus should be placed on the middle school environment.

Further, the effect of ability grouping was found to significantly differentiate high bonding schools from lower bonding schools. While previous research indicates that ability grouping is pervasive throughout every level of primary and secondary education, this study finds it to only impact the school bond in high schools (see: Epple, et. al., 2002; Gamoran, 1992; Oakes, et. al., 1992).

Finally, the school bond for African Americans was found to be weakened when attending schools which hand down higher numbers of suspensions and expulsions. While this finding was unique to the 5th grade results, it lends support to the initial hypothesis.

The U.S. Department of Education, Office of Civil Rights has continually noted African American students are disproportionately punished in the public school system. An early study by Patricia Jenkins (1995) indicated that students perceive differential treatment of Whites and non-Whites in the public school system, particularly in the enforcement of school rules. When students feel as if they are a target of unequal punishment, those students experience alienation and begin to develop an adversarial relationship with teachers and school administrators (see: Mulvey & Cauffman, 2001).

In short, this study found support for a number of the initial research hypotheses, and in turn, support for previous research in the field. Though some support was found for the initial hypotheses, there were other unanticipated findings of note.

Other Notable Findings
It was noted that African American males experienced higher bonds than females in 8th and 11th grade. This is counter to previous research indicating African American males experience difficulty navigating the academic environment. In part this finding, coupled with the finding that schools with higher minority enrollment experience higher average bonds to school, could be unique to this state and the patterns of busing. When African American students remain in their community schools instead of being bused to suburban schools, males experience stronger bonds to school. This, however, does not explain the 11th grade findings.

At a more basic level, it is possible that racial identity is at the heart of this finding of gender differences in African American students. Gilligan (1992) indicated that African American females are placed in a difficult position in the development of their racial identity. In order to 'do school' these females have to conform to traditional expectations, and blend in with other students. Race, being a salient factor in the school environment, may actually negatively impact a female more so than a male. If teachers expect African Americans to be less successful in school, it would be difficult for an African American female to 'do school', since her race will preclude her from becoming invisible within the school setting.

This concept is very different for males. Males are expected to be more mischievous so when a boy acts out, it is less out of character and thus less stigmatized. Again, research has indicated teachers expect less from African American males as opposed to White males. So, when African American males are successful, it is likely to be greeted with much praise from teachers. This positive affirmation may then strengthen the school bond.

Further addressing Gilligan's (1992) work, is the negative consequences experience by females when they use drugs and/or associate with delinquent peers. The negative impact of drug use and delinquent peer association is stronger for females than for males. This suggests when girls act against traditional gender role expectations, by engaging in drug use or associating with delinquent peers, the consequences to their reputation are more severe. This isolation can weaken their bond to school.

One of the most unexpected findings, though one that requires further discussion, is the improvement in average school bonding found in a school when that school has a large enrollment of students in poverty. One particular fact unique to this state is the high proportion of students who attend private or parochial schools. This flight out of public school is in part due to the practice of busing in the state to maintain diversity across schools in the largest, most populated county in the state. Students in the 8th grades are bussed out of the suburban areas and into city schools.

It is at this point when a number of students leave public school for private or parochial schools. Many parents feel uncomfortable with their children attending schools in an urban area, particularly when it is not their local community school.

An exploratory analysis indicated that the majority of schools with strong bonds and high poverty students are found in the more rural region of the state. This may indicate that the positive effect of poverty on the average bond in a school is actually predominantly in rural areas which are comprised of community schools that do not employ busing. This may indicate that this finding is not so much an effect of poverty, rather than measurement error. There may be an unmeasured factor of rural community schools, rather than schools with a high proportion of poverty, which improves the school bond. However, additional research is necessary to confirm this supposition.

Overall, these findings indicate that the school bond remains a predominantly individual phenomenon. The majority of the explanatory power comes from the individual-level characteristics primarily in the 8th and 11th grade. While the 5th grade models were weak, the findings present a first attempt to model the school bond in elementary school.

Grade Level Differences in Process of School Bonding

There are some notable changes in the population demographics between the samples. While certain measures are not comparable, there are others which are worth mentioning. In comparison to the 5th grade, the 8th grade sample has a higher proportion of African American students; an increase of 7 percent. One potential explanation for this could be the use of bussing measures by the state to promote diversity throughout at least one county in the state. This increased proportion of

African American students in the middle school population could be because white, suburban students enter private schools, rather than be bused to the public schools in the city. In the county in question, there are many private schools available to families who which to take their children out of public education.

There is also a marked reduction in the percent of students residing with both parents. This suggests that roughly an additional 15 percent of the 8th students, as compared to the 5th grade students, may have experienced the loss of a parent in the home; whether it be through divorce, death, prison or another means, fewer students in the 8th grade sample are living with both parents. The percent of students residing with both parents remains the same in both the 8th and 11th grade samples.

The 11th grade sample, however, reflects fewer African American students. There was roughly a 10 percent decline in African American populations in the schools. At the same time, however, this 11th grade sample reflects a marginal increase in Non-African American minority enrollment. The average grade point average is slightly higher in the 11th grade than the 8th grade sample, while the average level of delinquency, drug use and association with delinquent peers is lower in the 11th grade in comparison to the 8th grade. This suggests that the 11th grade sample is less delinquent than the 8th grade sample, while exhibiting a slightly lower average bond to school.

Differences in Schools

High schools were found to be the largest schools, enrolling roughly 1,250 students on average, and to exact more punishment than elementary and middle schools. The use of ability grouping was found to be uniform across elementary, middle and high schools. Previous research has indicated that this is a common practice across all levels of schooling, though the practice is rarely reported (Ogbu, 2000).

The elementary schools in the sample, though the smallest in average enrollment, report a greater concentration of students in poverty as well as a greater average minority enrollment in comparison to middle and high schools. The high schools, however, report the smallest proportion of students receiving free or reduced lunch in comparison to elementary and middle schools. This suggests that a portion of the marginalized population is no longer present in this 11th grade sample. While the reason for this decline is speculation, it must be noted that students are able to voluntarily drop out of school in the

10th grade. Nevertheless, there is a clear decline in the population of African American students (as noted in the section above) as well as a smaller proportion of students receiving free or reduced lunch in comparison to the 5th and 8th grade samples.

Differences in Effects Across Grades

Gender proved to have a different impact on the school bond across the grade levels. In the 5th grade sample the effect of being male was found to improve the bond to school; however, by the time a student reached the 8th and into the 11th grade, the effect of being male was found to reduce the school bond. There were also certain gender-specific effects found to differ by grade level.

In the 5th grade, the effect of residing in a two-parent home was found to be stronger for females. Developmental literature would support this finding suggesting girls at this age have stronger attachment to their parents rather than school. However, the same effect was noted for 11th grade females. Further, drug use and delinquent peer associations was found to have a stronger negative impact on the female school bond than the male school bond.

In the 8th and 11th grade the effect of being African American was significantly impacted by one's gender. In both the 8th and 11th grade, African American males experienced stronger bonds to school than African American females. Race, however, was not found to have a significant impact in the 5th grade gender specific models.

In the 5th grade the effect of being either African American or Non-African American minority improved a student's bond to school, though these race effects disappear by the time students reach the 8th grade. Race was not found to have a consistent impact on the school bond in either the 8th or 11th grade. There were certain race-specific differences found to differ between grades. The effects of residing with both parents and parent's education on the school bond were found to be significantly lower for 8th grade non-African American minorities, while the effect of parents education on school bonding is weaker for 11th grade African American students.

In the 5th grade, older students were found to experience significantly higher levels of school bonding. This, however changes by the time students reach middle school. In the 8th grade as well as in the 11th grade age was found to significantly reduce the bond to school. Further, grade point average was not found to have a significant impact on the elementary school bond; however, it was found to significantly improve the bond to school in both the 8th and 11th grade.

Finally, individual drug use was noted to weaken the bond in both the 8th and 11th grades, however, not in the 5th grade. The same pattern was noted for delinquent behavior.

This analysis suggests that the model, particularly in the 8th and 11th grades, is able to explain a significantly larger proportion of the variation in school bonding compared to the 5th grade. While the proportion of variation explained in the 5th grade is very small, it remains an avenue for future research.

Further, this research contended that in order to look at the student-school bond, contextual variables must be examined to provide a larger picture than individual differences in predicting the school bond. While these variables did not explain a large proportion of difference between schools, the models did provide informative and interesting results and indicated that the impact of the school context on the school bond is unique to each grade.

As students progressed through their educational endeavors, a greater proportion of variation in school bonding was explained by between schools differences. The 5th grade model, which presented the lowest proportion of explained variation in school bonding by between school differences, found no school-level direct effect on school bonding; there were, however, notable interaction effects. African American students who attend schools with a higher proportion of other African American students experience a stronger bond to school; however, this school bond for African Americans is weakened when attending schools which hand down higher numbers of suspensions and expulsions. Further, elementary school students who use drugs are more ostracized when they attend schools with lower proportions of drug use.

The 8th grade model was able to explain a bit more variation in school bonding with between school measures than the 5th grade model. For the first time, school contextual variables were found to have a direct effect on the average school bond within a school. Larger middle schools experience a lower mean level of school bonding. Schools that report a high proportion of punishment were found to experience *lower* average levels of school bonding among students in that school. Schools with higher minority populations and higher proportions of students on free and reduced lunch experience an *above* average level of student-school bonding at the 8th grade level.

Other interaction effects were found to be significant, though the significant interaction effects from the 5th grade did not remain significant in the 8th grade. Instead, 8th grade males are less likely to be bonded to a school, and, in those schools with higher minority enrollment, the average male-school bond is even further reduced. Also, students in schools where there is an above average proportion of students punished see a decline in the positive GPA-school bond relationship.

High school context yet again differs from the elementary and middle school environment. For the first time, the effect of ability grouping was found to significantly differentiate high bonding schools from lower bonding schools. The effect of the proportion of students in poverty, as in the 8th grade, continues to improve a school's average level of bonding. Unlike the 8th grade models, variables such as size and minority enrollment have no significant impact. Further, unlike the 5th and 8th grade models, the school context was not found to moderate the relationship between any individual-level variables and the school bond.

This study suggests that while the school context provides an additional level of explanation, the school bond remains predominantly influenced by one's individual background. A transition takes place between elementary and middle school which leads to a transformation of the school bond. Those factors which influence an individual's bond to school in the 5th grade change by the time a student reaches the 8th and subsequently the 11th grade. Further, at the elementary school level, the proposed model had very little explanatory power indicating the school context provided little additional understanding towards the school bond.

Those factors which previous research has identified as having a negative impact on school connectedness: gender, race and age, were found to promote a prosocial bond to school at the elementary school level when controlling for delinquency and association with delinquent peers. By the time a student reaches the 8th grade, however, these factors have fallen in line with previous research in the area. This indicates a need for further research in the area of school connectedness among elementary school populations and the development of an elementary school model that is able to explain a greater proportion of variation in the school bond.

By the time a student reaches the 8th grade, a transition has occurred which has changed the impact of individual background on the school bond. The effect of gender and age are more in line with previous research findings, though the effect of race was found to differ by gender. There are more avenues for involvement in the school and students are developing stronger bonds to their peers. As the school context begins to explain more between-school variation, the individual-level variables explain a greater proportion of variation in the individual school bond. There was more support for the initial research hypotheses in the 8th grade than noted in the 5th grade. In addition, school context has a more significant impact on the middle school bond. This may indicate that the school context is more salient to the school bond during the time of transition in the middle school environment. If this be the case, future research may also want to include measures of stress, depression and isolation to add an additional dimension to the study of school bonding.

In short, this study addressed the issue of school bonding from elementary to high school. The results of this analysis have implications for future policy and practices in the public school system as well as for parents of school aged children. In the following section, these policy implications will be discussed and recommendations will be made for schools and parents to hopefully maximize a student's bond to school.

Policy Implications

Acknowledging that this research was conducted with cross-sectional data, and causality cannot be identified, there are still certain policy recommendations that can be made. Schools should continue to fund school-based activities including sports and music. While this study did not disentangle the individual components of the social bond, the reliability analysis supports the school bond measure in the 8th and 11th grades indicates that involvement correlates well with the other components of the school bond. When schools provide students with activities which develop their skills, promote their talents, and improve collegiality between individuals, it is likely to improve the overall bonding within the school. Through school activities, students get the experience of working together as a team, and negotiating interpersonal interactions with the broader student population. Moreover, school activities provide students with a type of school or social capital which further attaches them to the school, the school environment, and each other. If the goal is to enhance the school bond, cutting school activities may be harmful to interpersonal student interactions, individual student development, as well as the overall school climate.

In addition, while the use of ability grouping may be important for the schools, when students reach the high school level it begins to harm the student-school bond. This academic stratification that comes from ability grouping may work for the high academic track students, but the stigmatization of low academic track continues to alienate students within a school. This stratification between academically talented students and those who are not as talented becomes more apparent in schools that employ ability grouping. Previous research indicates that those schools that do not employ ability grouping have a stronger sense of community (see Epple, et. al., 2002; Gammoran, 1992). When students are not experiencing the stratification of ability grouping, their focus is less on rankings and thus more willing to focus on community building within the school environment. This factor tends to be most salient at the high school level. When possible, high school administrators should attempt to find a less stigmatizing method of grouping students in the current hierarchical fashion.

By the time a student reaches the 11th grade, or at the age of 16, he or she is legally able to drop out of school. Thus, it can be assumed that the students who are present in the 11th grade choose to be there. While the traditional indicators of social strain within a school, such as high minority enrollment and high proportions of students on the free and reduced lunch program were not found to impact the mean level of school bonding in the hypothesized direction, the use of ability grouping within a high school and the academic stratification that results could be the cause of social strain in high school. Offering curriculum alternatives such as vocational programs or professional apprenticeships/co-ops for academic credit may provide an alternative academic tracking that caters to the goals of students and produce a less academically stratified learning environment. Though there are specific schools in the state which cater to vocational education, all public schools may want to provide career counseling as well as college counseling, particularly when students enter the 11th grade. Many schools are willing to mentor students to get into college, but few offer similar services for students who will go directly into the workforce.

Further, middle schools may help to foster the student-school bond by reducing school enrollment. Large schools and large classrooms are stressful for both the teacher and the students. In large classrooms, teachers become managers more so than educators and students do not get the individualized attention or mentorship they may need. Particularly when students are struggling through adolescence, a large school environment could produce another level of strain which further alienates students from peers and adult authority figures. The transition from a nurturing elementary school experience into a much larger middle school environment is a stressor on the school bond. If a child is coming from an elementary school environment where he or she feels nurtured, it is likely that the larger school enrollment of middle school will create strain as these students forge prosocial relationships with new peers, faculty and administrators. If the teacher-student ratio does not increase proportionately with the enrollment size, it is likely that larger class sizes makes the development of a teacher-student bond more difficult. While school officials may not have say regarding the school enrollment, these officials should be considering ways to improve the student-teacher interaction so that students can bond with faculty and administration regardless of school enrollment. One such opportunity might be during an orientation session for students to their new school, breaking into smaller groups during such an activity might give a nervous student an adult ally when the first day of school arrives.

Finally, while schools may take a 'get tough' approach to discipline infractions, this may not be the most effective policy to foster bonding among the students. While this may be most salient for middle schools, previous research indicates it may be a beneficial task for all schools. Nevertheless, schools should begin to study how they carry out punishment on the student body. In some schools, swift, certain, and severe punishment may be effective in keeping students in line. For others, however, discipline may be a barrier between the students and their educational endeavors. Schools must be clear that the punishment that is being handed down is not only deserved, but is fair for a given infraction. This can significantly impact the students' perception of teachers and administration within the school leading to a potential increase in the average level of bonding found in a school. When students are vested in the reality that if they are to break a rule any one of them could be punished, it reduces the perception that a particular student would be the target of a faculty member or administrator.

In summary, while schools must be standardized in terms of curriculum, that does not mean that programming and school-based activities cannot account for the population represented in that school. Moreover, schools will benefit from working with their students to increase the student-school bond, seeing a reduction in the level of delinquency and substance use among students in the school.

While the school context provides an important piece to the school bonding puzzle, it is still only a small piece. As the HLM results across all 3 grade levels indicate, the school bond remains predominantly an individual phenomenon.

There are a number of factors that cannot be influenced by policy; an individual's race, gender, family structure, and parent's educational attainment, for example. However, there are a few things that can be suggested to assist parents and students in developing positive prosocial bonds to school.

First, while divorce is a reality in our society, parents can work together to provide a united message about the importance of education for their children. Reinforcing the importance of education in both homes provides the child with consistency with regards to academic success. In addition, as difficult as it may be, parents could attempt to be present at school functions, provide academic resources in both homes and present a uniform message regarding homework and grades, again reinforcing the importance of school and the educational experience. When parents are present at school events and school activities involving their child, it not only reinforces the parent-child bond, but also validates the student's involvement in school improving the student-school bond.

Parents can also be present in the life of their children by knowing who their kids are hanging out with and what they are doing. Of particular note inquiring about how their child is doing in school and within the school environment. A parent can make a substantial difference in the life of their child simply by monitoring how he or she is doing. Parental involvement can potentially lead to higher grade point averages and lower levels of participation in delinquency, drug use and association with delinquent peers. All of which will improve a student's bond to school. Delinquency research consistently identifies association with delinquent peers as the strongest predictor of juvenile delinquency. If parents know their child's friends it might make a significant impact on their child's delinquent behavior and help ensure that the student is successful in the school environment.

At the same time, schools can also help reduce the effects of these characteristics by encouraging involvement of noncustodial parents, and assisting youth whose parents are less well-educated and struggle navigating the educational system. One problem that many parents face is one of inexperience. If a child comes from parents who have not experienced the American educational system, these parents may not be comfortable in or even know how to find the ways to ensure their child's success. This is further aggravated if the parent or parents are not fluent in the English language. Schools may be able to assist these parents by helping to educate parents about the demands and expectations of the school curriculum.

Limitations to this Research
Though this study provides informative results regarding the school bond, it was not without pitfalls. One weakness of this study is the data was not gathered for the sole purpose of this analysis. As such there was no measure of belief, the fourth component of Hirschi's social bond, which could be utilized in this study. Thus, the school bond measure in this study is not complete as proposed in Hirschi's control theory, and the reliability for the constructs are lower for African Americans than any other race/ethnic group. In addition, the data used for this analysis were cross-sectional, so for many variables, it is impossible to determine directionality.

Future research in this area should attempt to tailor a study which could follow students across time to determine the transitions and trajectories for change in the school bond through the academic life course of students. Previous research has indicated the transition from elementary to middle school is an intensely difficult time for students, and a better understanding of this transition may be a key to the school experience for both elementary and middle school students.

Further, this study only included public schools. While the sample included certain vocational schools, no private, parochial, or charter schools were included in this analysis. Another interesting research question would be to compare the school bond across public, private, parochial and charter schools to effectively capture differences between schools.

In addition, while the hierarchical (HLM) analysis in this study provides informative findings regarding the impact of the school context on school bonding, this method of analysis did not allow for the analysis of indirect effects. This is a limitation of the current research, particularly noting that school bonding was found to be predominantly influenced by individual characteristics. Future research may want to address the issues of both direct and indirect effects on the school bond. A structural equation model, accounting for both direct and indirect effects may provide a more complete picture of the process of school bonding.

Suggestions for the Future

A number of interesting results were noted in this study of the impact of individual and school context on school bonding. First, this study, unlike previous research, found African American males to exhibit a stronger bond to school than other males. This is counter to a body of previous research suggesting that African American males experience the most difficulty navigating the educational experience. One possible explanation for this is the unique pattern of busing present in the northernmost county of this state, which keeps African American students in their own community schools while busing in white, suburban students for middle school. Future research may want to address the salience of race in elementary and secondary schools, and what that racial identity does to an individual's experience in school, specifically as it may vary by gender. While previous research has addressed issues of races in terms of inequality within a school, additional research is needed to understand what is different about White's, African American's or non-African American minority's experiences in the educational setting.

Another major finding of this study is identifying the unique experience of elementary school as it relates to the school bond. Previous research has provided a limited explanation of the elementary school bond, and this research indicates that the model that predicts the school bond in middle and high school students is not sufficient in explaining the elementary school bond. While the proportion of variation explained in the 5th grade is very small, it remains an avenue for future research. The elementary school bond, as explained by individual-level variables, is not significantly captured by this model. In fact, a number of the findings were in direct opposition to the initial research hypotheses. Future research should analyze the differences in the elementary school bond, specifically what is salient in the elementary school experience that is not captured in this model in order to provide a better understanding of the school bonding mechanism in the 5th grade.

Further, since the proposed model was able to explain a greater proportion of variation in school bonding in the 8th and 11th grade than in the 5th grade, this finding suggests that the process of school bonding changed from 5th grade to 8th grade. This transformation in school bonding that occurs between 5th and 8th grade provides an avenue for future research. Additional research should focus on identifying this change in bonding between grades.

Another key finding is the limited importance of the school context on a school bond. Overall, there was little variation to be explained by between school measures. The school context, however, was found to be most significant to the middle school bond. School-level variables not only impact the mean level of bonding within a school, but also impact an individual-level variable's effect on a student's bond. It must be noted, however, that these samples are large and that it is possible some of these significant effects occur by chance. Nevertheless, this finding may indicate that the school context is more salient to the school bond during the time of transition in the middle school environment. Previous research has indicated this transition to be a stressful time for adolescents. If this be the case, future research may also want to include measures of stress, depression and isolation to assess these dimensions of school bonding.

Endnotes

[1] This theoretical paradigm has also been utilized by Jenkins (1995), Cernkovich and Girodano (1992), and Wiatrowski and Anderson (1987), to explain school delinquency.

[2] Maddox and Prinz (2003) expand Cernkovich and Giordano's (1992) attachment to teachers to include all school personnel. Thus, the Maddox and Prinz (2003) definition of school personnel includes educators, staff (such as counselors, mentors, coaches, etc.), and administration.

[3] It is important to note that attachments to parents, as well as to peers, are not included in one's attachment to school. Peer and parental attachment represent qualitatively different bonds than those of an attachment to school (see Hirschi, 1969).

[4] Additional support for Hirschi (1969) and school bonding can be found beginning on page 47 of this chapter under the *Delinquency* section of the literature review.

[5] That is not to say that all public schools carry expectations of the middle class. Certain schools specialize in providing vocational programs or music and the arts for those students who find this modality of education more appealing than a traditional public school environment.

[6] In addition to the main teacher, other adults such at teacher's aides or parent volunteers may also be present in the classroom. While this may add to the structure of the classroom, the teacher still has the primary role of educator.

[7] Pro-social in this context can be defined as a behaviors that are helpful rather than harmful to others.

[8] A November, 2003 report from the National Center for Education Statistics reports Hispanics have the highest drop out rate across racial/ethnic categories at 7.5 percent; however, African Americans continue to have a markedly high drop out rate (5.3%) compared to White students (3.6%).

[9] As a caveat, it is important to mention that Cernkovich and Giordano (1992) acknowledged that their female population was less delinquent than the males which could have a significant impact on this particular finding.

[10] The finding that the most significant component for the social bond for males is involvement was also supported by Williams and McGee (1991).

11. The time frame of the survey questions supports the temporal order that past year delinquency could impact the current student-school bond.

12. Status frustration refers to the emotions that confront an individual when their level of deprivation prevents them from achieving status in society (see Cohen, 1955).

13. If teachers are frustrated with their classroom, they too may withdraw and be less compassionate and available for the students. When teachers are not accessible to the students, students are not as likely to be attached. This is analogous to the weak attachments that are formed when a parent is not available to their child.

14. The term "in school" includes incidents that occur inside the school building, on the school property (i.e.: playground, athletic fields), or school bus during the school day (see School Crime and Safety, 2001; Appendix C).

15. While this seems to be a high rate of victimization within the school, juveniles of school age were victims of approximately 1.1 million crimes outside of the school setting (School Crime and Safety, 2001). While victimization is higher outside of the school environment, school aged students are still faced with a reasonable chance of victimization while on school property.

16. An article from the *New York* Times, written by a student from Littleton, CO., contends that drawing on a piece of paper can get a student expelled under the new zero-tolerance policies. Thus, students are entering the classroom with an increased sense of concern that they will be punished for behavior that was at one time acceptable (Black, 2001).

17. This can only be tested comparing the 8th and 11th grades due to measurement differences in the survey instrument between 5th, 8th, and 11th grades.

18. The content of the survey is similar however, the questions were written in an age-appropriate way. Specifically, the 5th grade survey was written at a 5th grade reading level with questions related to the 5th grade experience. The 8th and 11th grade surveys were written in the same age-specific manner.

19. There were checks in the survey to ensure the validity of the data. Questions were in place in the survey asking about the use of fictitious drugs. Those students who respond in the affirmative to fictitious drug use were removed from the data. This was an attempt to reduce falsified data. Clearly, if a student reported using a fictitious drug their self-reported drug use was in question.

20. The question asks if the respondent is a "boy" or "girl" on the 5th grade survey.

21. For 5th grade, the students can choose 9 years or younger, 10, 11, or 12 years old. For the 8th grade, students can respond as 13 years or younger, 14, 15, or 16 years or older. Finally, the 11th grade can respond 15 years or younger, 16, 17, 18 years old, or 19 years or older.

22. The 5th grade survey only asks if the student was "White", "Black or African American", "Hispanic or Latino", "Asian", or "Other".

[23.] The *living with both parents* variable for the 5th grade asks if the student "lives with both parents (including stepparents)".

[24.] The final coding scheme for each variable was as follows: 5 'completed grade school or less', 10 'some high school', 12 'completed high school', 14 'some college', 16 'completed college', 19 'graduate or professional school after college'.

[25.] Again, this is a different measure for the 5th grade. The concepts are the same, asking if any of the respondent's friends "smoke cigarettes", "drink alcohol", or "smoke marijuana". The variables are each measured dichotomously, so that 1 represents "yes" and 2 represents "no". The 5th grade, like the others, is an additive scale so that the higher the score on the scale the greater the association with delinquent peers.

[26.] The 5th grade school bond variable consisted of just two of the four bonding measures: attachment and commitment. There was no measure of involvement for the 5th grade and the survey was also lacking a valid belief measure applicable to rules in schools.

[27.] While each of the surveys asked students if they believed that most people are punished if they break the law, there is a concern regarding face validity with the operationalization of 'belief' as an element of school bonds in this context. That is to say that this variable is not specific to the school environment, school-specific rules and norms and as such does not represent a belief found in a social bond with school.

[28.] There was an additional classification for "I don't know" which was recoded as missing for this analysis.

[29.] The values of 1 and 5 for these variables were chosen to maintain consistency with the rest of the scale where the variable values range from 1 to 5.

[30.] Since these surveys were conducted from January to June of 2000, each of these categories represent valid potential answers. The students would have been enrolled in school for a long enough period of time that the student could have potentially attended an event at least once a week during the survey period.

[31.] These schools were then matched with the 115 schools sampled in the state school survey. Therefore, not all the schools surveyed by the E&S Survey (i.e.: Charter Schools) were included in this study.

[32.] The lower proportion of elementary schools in the sample is due to the sampling procedure of the individual-level student surveys. There are a greater proportion of elementary schools in the state than middle or high schools due to the grade configuration of schools. Not all elementary schools in the state contain 5th grade students. Thus, while 52 percent of all the elementary schools within the state were sampled, it was due to grade configuration and not to the schools' refusal to participate. In short, there were more elementary schools in the state but not included in this study since these schools did not include a 5th grade class.

33 This enrollment figure does not account for the number of students who may have dropped out, relocated to or from the school, or students whose educational privileges at a given school were terminated due to behavioral problems.

34 This is not an exact proportion since some of these students were disciplined multiple times.

35 For clarity, the proposed individual-level variables were placed initially into an OLS regression model to have a clear idea of how these variables predict school bonds. This step is the first stage of the Hierarchical Linear Model, but is not reported, thus in order to be thorough these models were run separately so the results could be presented.

36 Substituting the mean for the missing cases is analogous to weighting the variable around the mean. Therefore, with less than 4% missing data, this is an acceptable alternative to list or pairwise deletion techniques (Little & Rubin, 1986).

37 The subscript j allows each school to have a unique intercept and slope, thus the slopes will vary across schools.

38 These slopes (β's) will vary, and it is that variation that will be explained in the level-2 (school-level) models.

39 Not centering the dichotomous variables of gender and race assumes that each of these schools have the same means on these variables (Byrk & Raudenbush, 2002; Arnold, 1992). In fact, there is very little variation in the means of these dichotomous variables across schools in all three samples, thus the assumption made by not centering these variables is not distorting the sample or model interpretations.

40 The cross-level effects can also be thought of as interaction effects. The level-1, or individual-level effect depends upon the value of a level-2, or school-level, predictor.

41 Though variables were created to measure the mean effect that delinquency and individual drug use within a school has on the level of school bonding, utilizing this methodology the level-1 predictors for individual drug use and delinquency can remain randomly varying and centered around the group mean at level-2 (school-level) to calculate the same estimate without including another variable in the analysis.

42 Again, given the clear original metrics of the school-level variables, the interpretations will be meaningful without centering.

43 There was not a sufficient sample size to run a separate analysis of non-African American minorities. See Table 1.

44 *p<.05; ** p<.01; ***p<.001

45 Even though certain predictors in these 5th, 8th, and 11th grade analyses are significantly associated with one another, none of the correlations are of significant magnitude to create problems of multicollinearity in the regression analyses. A collinearity analysis produced no variance inflation factor greater than 1.8. The level of association among the independent variables in this

analysis is not sufficient to produce uncertain or uninterpretable regression coefficients.

46. Equation for the Chow Test: F= ([SSE$_T$-(SSE$_M$-SSE$_F$)]/p) / [SSE$_M$+SSE$_F$] / (n-2p); where SSE is the residual sum of squares for the total model, the male only model, and the female only model, and p=number of predictors in the model (Chow, 1960).

47. *p<.05; ** p<.01; ***p<.001

48. N= 5503

49. *p<.05; ** p<.01; ***p<.001

50. N= 5503

51. It must be noted here that the dependent variable in this analysis, while still an estimate of the student-school bond, is now interpreted as the mean level of school bonding for an average student within a given school, rather than the change in the individual school bond as was the case in the OLS regression models.

52. * p<0.05; ** p<0.010; ***p<0.001

53. School N = 43; Individual N = 5503

54. Results of the Chow test are as follows: White v. African American F=337.00; White v. Non-African American minority F=326.13; African American v. Non-African American minority F=113.76. All of these F-statistics are significant, indicating that the models significantly differ from one another.

55. Again, all but 1 of the schools in the 8th grade sample self-identified as a middle school. The one outlier self-identified as a high school.

56. School N= 31; Individual N= 5018

57. * p<0.05; ** p<0.010; ***p<0.001

58. School N= 31; Student N=3937

59. *p<.05; ** p<.01; ***p<.001

60. *p<.05; ** p<.01; ***p<.001

61. Results of the Chow test are as follows: White v. African American F=337.00; White v. Non-African American minority F=326.13; African American v. Non-African American minority F=113.76. All of these F-statistics are significant, indicating that the models significantly differ from one another.

62. *p<.05; ** p<.01; ***p<.001

63. * p<0.05; ** p<0.010; ***p<0.001

64. School N= 31; Student N=3901

65. Again, all but 1 of the schools in the 8th grade sample self-identified as a middle school. The one outlier self-identified as a high school.

References

Acia, E.A. & K.C. Connors. (1998) "Gender Differences in ADHD?". *Developmental and Behavioral Pediatrics*, 19: 77-83.

Advancement Project/Civil Rights Project. (2000). Opportunities suspended: The devastating consequences of zero tolerance and school discipline policies. Cambridge, MA: Harvard University.

Agnew, R. (1993). "Why do they do it? "An examination of the intervening mechanisms between 'social control' variables and delinquency." *Journal of Research in Crime and Delinquency*, 30(3): 245-266.

Agnew, R. (1985). "Social Control Theory and Delinquency: A Longitudinal Test." *Criminology*, 23: 47-61.

Agresti, A. & B. Findlay. (1997). *Statistical Methods for the Social Sciences*. Upper Saddle River, NJ: Prentice-Hall.

Akers, R.L. (1997). *Criminological Theories: Introduction and Evaluation*. Los Angles, CA: Roxbury Press.

Akers, R.L., M.D. Krohn, L. Lanza-Kaduce, & M. Radosevich. (1979). "Social learning and deviant behavior: A specific test of a general theory." *American Sociological Review*, 44: 635-655.

Altenbaugh, R. J., D.E. Engel & D.T Martin. (1995). *Caring For Kids: A Critical Study Of Urban School Leavers*. London: The Falmer Press.

Alvarez, A., & Bachman, R. (1997). "Predicting the fear of assault at school and while going to and from school in an adolescent population." *Violence and Victims*, 12: 69-86.

Alwin, D.F. & L.B. Otto. (1977). "High school context effects on aspirations". *Sociology of Education*, 50(4): 259-273.

Arnold, C. L. (1992). "An introduction to hierarchical linear models." *Measurement and Evaluation in Counseling and Development*, 25: 58-90.

Arum, R. (2000). "Schools and communities: Ecological and institutional dimensions." *Annual Review of Sociology*, 26: 395-418.

Ascher, C. (1994). "Gaining Control of Violence in the Schools: A View from the Field." ERIC Digest No. 100. ERIC Clearinghouse on Urban Education, New York, NY; National Education Association, Washington, DC. Center for the Revitalization of Urban Education. (ERIC Document Reproduction Service No. ED 377 256).

Astone, N & S.S. McLanahan (1991). "Family Structure, Parental Practices and High School Completion." *American Sociological Review*, 56(3): 309-320.

Astor, R.A., & H.A. Meyer (2001). The conceptualization of violence-prone school subcontexts: Is the sum of the parts greater than the whole? *Urban Education*, 36(3): 374-399.

Bachman, R. & R. Peralta (2002). "The relationship between drinking and violence in an adolescent population: Does gender matter." *Deviant Behavior: An Interdisciplinary Journal*, 23:1-19.

Becker, H. (1963). *Outsiders" Studies in the Sociology of Deviance.* New York: Free Press.

Berndt, T. (1986). "Friends' influence on adolescents' adjustment to school." *Developmental Psychology*, 15: 608-616.

Billingsley, A. (1968). *Black Families in White America.* Englewood Cliffs, NJ: Prentice Hall.

Bowditch, C. (1993). Getting rid of troublemakers: High school disciplinary procedures and the production of dropouts. *Social Problems*, 40: 493–507.

Bryant, A.L., J. Schulenberg, J.G. Bachman, P.M. O'Malley, & L.D. Johnston (2000). *Acting out and lighting up: Understanding the links among school misbehavior, academic achievement, and cigarette use.* (Monitoring the Future Occasional Paper No. 46). Ann Arbor, MI: The University of Michigan Institute for Social Research.

Burgess, R.L. (1979). "Family violence: Implications from evolutionary biology." In T. Hirschi (ed) *Understanding Crime* (pp: 91-101). Beverly Hills, CA: Sage.

Burke, P.J. & J. W. Hoelter. (1988). "Identity and sex-race differences in educational and occupational aspirations formation." *Social Science Research*, 17(1):29-47

Byrk, A.S., Lee, V.E., & Holland, P.B. (1993). *Catholic Schools and the Common Good*. Cambridge, MA: Harvard University Press.

Byrk, A.S. & Raudenbush, S.W. (2002). *Hierarchial Linear Models: Applications and Data Analysis Methods*. Newbury Park, CA: Sage.

Catalano, R. & J.D. Hawkins. (1996). "The social development model: A theory of antisocial behavior." In J.D. Hawkins (ed) *Delinquency and Crime: Current Theories* (pp: 149-197). Cambridge, England: Cambridge University Press.

Catalano, R., R. Kosterman, J.D. Hawkins, M.D. Newcomb, & R.D. Abbot. (1996). "Modeling the etiology of adolescent substance use: A test of the social development model." *Journal of Drug Issues*, 26: 429-455.

Canter, R. (1982). "Sex differences in self-report delinquency." *Criminology*, 20: 373-393.

Carmines, E. & R.A. Zeller. (1979). *Reliability and Validity Assessment*. Beverly Hills, CA: Sage.

Cernkovich, S. & P. Giordano (1992). "School Bonding and Race." *Criminology*, 30:261-291.

Chow, G.C. (1960). "Tests of equality between sets of coefficients in two linear relationships." *Econometrica*, 28: 591-606.

Chilton, R. J. & G.E. Marlke. (1972). "Family disruption and delinquent conduct: Multiple measures and the effect of subclassification." *American Sociological Review*, 37(1): 93-99.

Cloward, R. & L. Ohlin. (1961). *Delinquency and Opportunity*. Glencoe, Il: Free Press.

Cohen, A.(1955). *Delinquent Boys*. Glencoe, Illinois: Free Press.

Crosnoe, R., K.G. Erickson & S.M. Dornbusch. (2002). "Protective functions of family relationship and school factors on the deviant behaviors of adolescent boys and girls: Reducing the impact of risky friendships." *Youth & Society*, 33(4): 515-544.

Czikszentmihalyi, M. & R. Lawson. (1978). *Being Adolescent: Conflict and Growth in the Teenage Years*, New York: Basic Books.

Davis, J.E., & Jordan, W.J. (1994). "The effects of school context, structure, and experiences on African American males in middle and high schools." *Journal of Negro Education*, 63: 570–587.

Devine, J. (1996). *Maximum Security: The Culture of Violence in Inner-City Schools*. Chicago, IL: The University of Chicago Press.

Dornbusch, S.M., K.G. Erickson, J. Laird, & C.A. Wong. (2001). "The relation of family and school attachment to adolescent deviance in diverse groups and communities." *Journal of Adolescent Research*, 16(4): 396-422.

Edin, K. & L. Lein. (1997). *Making Ends Meet: How Single Mothers Survive Welfare and Low-Wage Work*. New York: Russell Sage Foundation.

Eggert L.L. & K.L. Kumpfer. (1997). "Drug abuse prevention for at-risk individuals." NIH Pub. #97-4115. Rockville, MD: DHHS, NIH, NIDA, Office of Science Policy and Communications.

Eggert, L.L., E.A. Thompson, J.R. Herting, L.J. Nicholas, & B.G. Dicker. (1994). "Preventing adolescent drug abuse and high school dropout through an intensive school-based social network development program." *American Journal of Health Promotion*, 8: 202-215.

Elliot, D., S. Ageton, & R. Cantor. (1985). "An Integrated Theoretical Perspective on Delinquent Behavior." *Journal of Research in Crime and Delinquency*, 16: 3-27.

Elliot, D. S., D. Huizinga, & S. S. Ageton. (1985) *Explaining Delinquency and Drug Use*. Sage; Beverley Hilly, CA.

Elliot, D. & H. Voss. (1974). *Delinquency and the Dropout*. Lexington, MA: Lexington Books.

Emery, R.E. (1982). "Interparental conflict and the children of discord and divorce." *Psychological Bulletin*, 92:310-30.

England, R.E., K.J Meier, & L.R. Fraga. (1988). "Barriers to equal opportunity: educational practices and minority students." *Urban Affairs Quarterly*, 23(4): 635-646.

Epple, D. E. Newlon, & R. Romano. (2002). "Ability tracking, school competition, and the distribution of educational benefits." *Journal of Public Economics*, 83(1): 1-48.

Epstein, J. & J. McPartland. (1976). "The Concept and Measurement of the Quality of School Life." *Educational Research Journal*, 13: 15-30.

Erikson, K.G., R. Crosnoe, & S.M. Dornbusch. (2000). "A social process model of adolescent deviance: Combining social control and differential association perspectives." *Journal of Youth and Adolescence*, 29(4): 395-425.

Farrington, D.P. (1992). "Criminal career research in the United Kingdom". *British Journal of Criminology*, 32(4): 521-536.

Fehrmann, R., Keith, T., & T. Rimers. (1987). "Home influence on school learning: Direct and indirect effects of parental involvement on high school grades." *Journal of Educational Research*, 80: 330-337.

Feldman, R. & R. Saletski. (1986). "Nonverbal communication in interracial teacher-student interaction." In R. Feldman (ed) *The Social Psychology of Education* (pp:115-131). Cambridge, MA: Cambridge University Press.

Free, M.D. (1994). "Religiosity, religious conservativism, bonds to school, ad juvenile delinquency among three categories of drug users." *Deviant Behavior*, 15: 151-170.

Freidman, J. & D. Rosenbaum. (1988). "Social Control Theory: the Salience of Components by Age, Gender, and Type of Crime." *Journal of Quantitative Criminology*, 4: 363-81.

Gamoran, A. (1992). "The Variable Effects of High School Tracking." *American Sociological Review*, 57:812-28.

Gilligan, C. (1991). "Women's Psychological Development: Implications for Psychotherapy" pp. 5-31 in *Women Girls & Psychotherapy: Reframing Resistance*. Gilligan, C., A.G. Rogers, & D.L. Tolman, eds. New York: Harrington Park Press.

Gottfriedson, D. (1986). "An Empirical Test of School-Based Environmental and Individual Interventions to Reduce the Risk of Delinquent Behavior." *Criminology*, 24: 705-31.

Gottfriedson, G. & D. Gottfriedson. (1985). *Victimization in Schools*. New York: Plenum Press.

Gove, W. & R. Crutchfield. (1982). "The Family and Juvenile Delinquency." *Sociology Quarterly*, 23: 301-19.

Hagan, J. (1989). "Micro- and macro-structures of delinquency causation and power-control theory of gender and delinquency." In S.F. Messner, M.D. Khron, & A.E. Liska (eds), *Theoretical Integration in the Study of Deviance and Crime* (pp: 213-228). Albany, NY: State University of New York Press.

Hawkins, J.D., R.F. Catalano, D.M. Morrison, J. O'Donnell, R.D. Abbott, & L.E. Day. (1992). "The Seattle social development project: Effects of the first four years on protective factors and problem behaviors." In J. McCord & R.E. Tremblay (eds), *Preventing Antisocial Behavior: Interventions from Birth Through Adolescence* (pp: 139-206). New York: Guilford Press.

Hawkins, J.D., J.W. Graham, E. Maguin, R. Abbott, K.G. Hill, & R.F. Catalano. (1997). "Exploring the effects of age of alcohol use initiation and psychosocial risk factors on subsequent alcohol misuse." *Journal of Studies on Alcohol*, 58: 280-290.

Heimer, K. & R.L. Matsueda. (1994). "Role-taking, role-commitment, and delinquency: A theory of differential social control." *American Sociological Review*, 59: 365-390.

Hellman, D.A., & Beaton, S. (1986). The pattern of violence in urban public schools: The influence of school and community. *Journal of Research in Crime and Delinquency*, 23: 102–127.

Hickman, M. & A. Piquero. (2001). "Exploring the relationship between gender, control balance, and deviance." *Deviant Behavior: An Interdisciplinary Journal*, 22: 323-351.

Hindelang, M.J. (1973). "Causes of delinquency: A partial replication and extension." *Social Problems*, 20: 471-487.

Hirschi, T. (1969). *Causes of Delinquency*. Berkeley, CA: University of California Press.

Howard, K.A., J. Flora, & M. Griffin. (1999). "Violence-prevention programs in schools: State of the science and implications for future research." *Applied Prevention & Psychology*, 8(3): 197-215.

Jenkins, P. (1997). "School delinquency and the school social bond." *Journal of Research in Crime and Delinquency*, 34: 337-67.

Jenkins, P. (1995). "School delinquency and commitment." *Sociology of Education*, 68(3): 221-239

Jenkins, P. (1993). *School Delinquency and the School Social Bond.* Dissertation Abstracts International, A: The Humanities and Social Sciences, 54 (3).

Kaeser, S.C. (1979). "Suspensions in school discipline". *Education and Urban Society*, 11: 465–484.

Kaufman, P., Chen, X., Choy, S.P., Ruddy, S.A., Fleury, J.K., Chandler, K.A., Rand, M.R., Klaus, P., & Planty, M.G. *Indicators of School Crime and Safety, 2000.* U.S. Departments of Education and Justice. NCES 2001-017/NCJ-184176. Washington, DC.:2000.

Kaufman, P., Chen, X., Choy, S.P., Peter, K., Ruddy, S.A., Miller, A.K., Fleury, J.K., Chandler, K.A., Planty, M.G, & Rand, M.R. *Indicators of School Crime and Safety, 2001.* U.S. Departments of Education and Justice. NCES 2002-113/NCJ-190075. Washington, DC.:2001.

Kelly, D.H. (2001). "Labeling and the consequences of wearing a delinquent label in a school setting." *Education*, 97(4): 371-380.

Kelly, D.H. (1978). "Track position, peer affiliation, and youth crime." *Urban Education*, 13(3): 397-406.

Kelly, D.H. (1976). "Track position, school misconduct, and youth deviance: A test of the interpretive effect of school commitment." *Urban Education*, 10: 20-27.

Kelly, D.H. (1975). "Status origins, track position, and delinquent involvement: A preliminary analysis." *Sociology and Social Research*, 58: 380-386.

Kelly, D.H. & R.W. Balch. (1971). "Social origins and school failure; A reexamination of Cohen's theory of working class delinquency". *Pacific Sociological Review*, 14: 413-430.

Khron, M. & J. Massey. (1980). "Social control and delinquent behavior: An examination of the elements of the social bond." *The Sociological Quarterly*, 21: 529-543.

Ketterlinus R.D., M.E. Lamb, & K.A. Nitz. (1994). "Adolescent Nonsexual and Sex-related Problem Behaviors: Their Prevalence, Consequences, and Co-Occurrence." In R.D. Ketterlinus & M.E. Lamb (eds.), *Adolescent Problem Behaviors*. Hillsdale, New Jersey: Lawrence Erlbaum Associates.

Kozol, J. (1967). Halls of darkness: Into the ghetto schools. *Harvard Educational Review*, 37(3): 379-407

Kozol, J. (1991). *Savage Inequalities: Children in America's Schools*. Chicago, IL: Perennial Press.

Lab, S. & J. Whitehead. (1992). *The School Environment and School Crime: Causes and Consequences*. Washington, D.C.: National Institute of Justice.

Lee, V. E. (2000). "Using Hierarchial Linear Modeling to Study Social Contexts: The Case of School Effects." *Educational Psychologist*, 35(2): 125-141.

Little, R.J.A. & D. B. Rubin. (1987). *Statistical Analysis with Missing Data*. New York: Wiley Publishing.

Loeber, R. (1996). Developmental continuity, change, and pathways in male juvenile problem behavior and delinquency. In J.D. Hawkins (Ed.), Delinquency and crime: Current theories. (pp. 1–27). Cambridge: Cambridge University Press.

Loeber, R., & Farrington, D.P. (1998). *Serious and violent juvenile offenders: Risk factors and successful interventions*. Thousand Oaks, CA: Sage.

Liska, A. & M. Reed. (1985). "Ties to conventional institutions and delinquency: Estimating reciprocal effects." *American Sociological Review*, 50: 547-60.

Maccoby, E.E. (1998). *The Two Sexes: Growing Up Apart, Coming Together*. Cambridge, MA: Belknap Press.

Maddox, S.J. & R.J. Prinz (2003). "School bonding in children and adolescents: Conceptualization, assessment, and associated variables." *Clinical Child and Family Psychology Review*, 6(1): 31-49.

Matsueda, R.L. & K. Heimer. (1987). "Race, family structure, and delinquency: A test of differential association and social control theories." *American Sociological Review* 52: 826-840.

Mazerolle, P., R. Brame, R. Paternoster, A. Piquero, & C. Dean. (2000). "Onset age, persistence, and offending versatility: Comparisons across gender." *Criminology*, 38: 1143-1172.

McCarthy, J.D., & D.R. Hoge (1987). "The social construction of school punishment: Racial disadvantage out of universalistic process." *Social Forces*, 65: 1101–1120.

McGee, Z.T. (1992). "Social class differences in the parental and peer influence on adolescent drug use." *Deviant Behavior*, 13: 349-372.

McCord, J. (1983). "Family Relationships and Crime." Pp 759-64 in *Encyclopedia of Crime and Justice*, ed. S.H. Kadish. New York: Free Press.

Merton, R.K. (1938). "Social structure and anomie." *American Sociological Review*, 3: 672-682.

Miller, W. (1958). "Lower-class culture as a generating milieu of gang delinquency." *Journal of Social Issues*, 14: 5-19.

Moffitt, T.E. (1993). Adolescence-limited and life-course persistent antisocial behavior: A developmental taxonomy. *Psychological Review*, 100: 674–701.

Morrison, G.M. & R. Skiba (2001). Predicting violence from school misbehavior: Promises and perils. *Psychology in the Schools*, 38(2): 173-184.

Mulvey, E.P. & E. Caufman (2001). "The inherent limits of predicting school violence." *American Psychologist*, 56(10): 797-802.

Murguia, E., Z.Y. Chen, & H.B. Kaplan. (1998). "A comparison of causal factors in drug use among Mexican Americans and non-Hispanic Whites." *Social Science Quarterly*, 79: 341-360.

Myers, D., A. Milne, K. Baker, & A. Ginsburg. (1987). "Student Discipline and High School Performance." *Sociology of Education*, 60: 18-33.

National School Lunch Program. (2000). http://www.fns.usda.gov/cnd/Lunch/AboutLunch/AboutNLSP.htm

National Center for Education Statistics. (2003). http://www.nces.ed.gov/pubs2004/dropout00-01/#4.

Nettles, S.M., W. Mucherah, & D.S. Jones. (2000). "Understanding resilience: The role of social resources." *Journal of Education for Students Placed at Risk (JESPAR)*, 5 (1-2): 47-60.

Nye, I. (1973). *Family Relationships and Delinquent Behavior*. Westport, CT: Greenwood Press.

Oakes, J. (1992). "Can tracking research inform practice? Technical, normative, and political considerations." *Educational Researcher, 21*(4), 12-21.

Oden, S. (1987). "The development of social competence in children." ERIC Digest No. 073. ERIC Clearinghouse on Urban Education, New York, NY; National Education Association, Washington, DC. Center for the Revitalization of Urban Education. (ERIC Document Reproduction Service No. ED 281610).

O'Donnell, J., J.D. Hawkins, & R.D. Abbott. (1995). "Predicting serious delinquency and substance use among aggressive boys." *Journal of Consulting and Clinical Psychology*, 63: 529-537.

Ogbu, J.U. (1990). "Minority education in comparative perspective." *Journal of Negro Education*, 59(1): 45-57.

Pestello, F.G. (1989). "Misbehavior in high school classrooms." *Youth and Society*, 20(3): 290-306

Pilgrim, C., A. Abbey, P. Hendrickson, & S. Lorenz. (1998). "Implementation and impact of a family-based substance use prevention program in rural communities." *The Journal of Primary Prevention*, 18: 341-361.

Polk, K., D. Frease, & F.L. Richmond. (1974). "Social Class, School Experience and Delinquency." *Criminology* 12: 84-95.

Polk, K. & D.S. Halferty. (1966). "Adolescence, Commitment, and Delinquency". *Journal of Research in Crime and Delinquency*, 3: 82-96.

Polk, K. & W. Shafer. (1972). *Schools and Delinquency*. Englewood Cliffs, NJ: Prentice Hall.

Porter, J.N. (1974). "Race, socialization and mobility in educational and early occupational attainment." *American Sociological Review*, 39(3): 303-316.

Prom-Jackson, S., S.T. Johnson, & M.B. Wallace. (1987). "Home environment, talented minority youth, and school achievement." *Journal of Negro Education*, 56: 111-121.

Rankin, J. (1980). "School Factors and Delinquency: Interactions by Age and Sex." *Sociology and Social Research* 64: 420-34.

Rankin, J. & L.E. Wells. (1991). "The preventive effects of the family on delinquency." In R. Berger (ed) *The Sociology of Juvenile Delinquency* (pp: 171-187). Chicago, IL: Nelson Hall.

Rees, D.I., L.M. Argys, & D. J. Brewer. (1996). "Tracking in the United States: Descriptive statistics from NELS." *Economics of Education Review*, 15 (1): 83-89.

Resnick, M.D., P. Bearman, R. Blum, & K. Bauman. (1997). "Protecting adolescents from harm." *JAMA,* 278(10), 823-832.

Rhodes, A. L. & A.J. Reiss, Jr. (1963) "Apathy, truancy and delinquency as adaptations to school failure." *Social Forces*, 48(9): 12-22.

Sampson, R.J. & J.H. Laub. (1993) *Crime in the Making: Pathways and Turning Points Through Life.* Cambridge, MA: Harvard University Press

Scarpitti, F. R. & A. L. Nielsen, (eds.). (1999). *Crime and Criminals: Contemporary and Classic Readings.* Los Angeles, CA: Roxbury Press.

Shafer, W.E., C. Olexa, & K.Polk (1972) "Programmed for social class: Tracking in high school." *Trans-Action*, 7(12): 39-46, & 63.

Simons-Morton, B.G., A. D. Crump, D. L. Haynie, & K.E. Saylor. (1999). Student-school bonding and adolescent problem behavior. *Health Education Research,* 14 (1): 99-107.

Skiba, R.J., Michael, R.S., Nardo, A.C., & Peterson, R. (2000). The color of discipline: Sources of racial and gender disproportionality in school punishment. Bloomington, IN: Indiana University, Indiana Education Policy Center.

Skiba, R.J., Peterson, R.L., & Williams, T. (1997). Office referrals and suspension: Disciplinary intervention in middle schools. *Education and Treatment of Children*, 20: 295–315.

Sprague, J., & Walker, H. (2000). Early identification and intervention for youth with antisocial and violent behavior. *Exceptional Children*, 66: 367–379.

Stinchcombe, A. (1978). *Theoretical Methods in Social History.* New York: Academic Press.

Sugai, G., Sprague, J.R., Horner, R.H., & Walker, H.M. (2000). Preventing school violence: The use of office discipline referrals to asses and monitor school-wide discipline interventions. *Journal of Emotional and Behavioral Disorders*, 8:94–101.

Taylor, M. & G. Foster. (1986). "Bad boys and school suspensions: Public policy implications for black males." *Sociological Inquiry*, 56: 498-506.

Taylor, R., L. Chatters, & V. Mays. (1988). "Parents, children, siblings, in-laws, and non-kin as sources for emergency assistance for black families." *Family Relations*, 37: 298-304.

Thorne, B. (1993). *Gender Play*. New Brunswick: Rutgers University Press.

Thornberry, T.P., M. Moore, & R.L. Christenson. (1985). "The effect of dropping out of high school on subsequent criminal behavior." *Criminology*, 23: 3-18.

Thornberry, T., A. Lizotte, M. Khron, M. Farnworth, & S.J. Jang. (1991). "Testing Interactional Theory: An examination of reciprocal causal relationships among family, school, and delinquency." *Journal of Criminal Law and Criminology*. 82: 3-35.

Tittle, C.R., M.J. Burke, & E.F. Jackson. (1986). "Modeling Sutherland's theory of differential association: toward an empirical clarification." *Social Forces*, 65(2): 405-432.

Tobin, T., & Sprague, J. (1999). "Alternative educational strategies: Reducing violence in school and the community." Journal of Emotional and Behavioral Disorders, 8: 129–200.

Tobin T.J., & Sugai, G. (1999). "Using sixth-grade school records to predict school violence, chronic discipline problems, and high school outcomes." *Journal of Emotional and Behavioral Disorders*, 7(1): 40-53.

Tobin, T., Sugai, G., & Colvin, G. (1996). "Patterns in middle school discipline records." *Journal of Emotional and Behavioral Disorders*, 4: 82–94.

Toby, J. (1998). "Getting serious about school discipline." *Public Interest,* 133:68-83.

Toby, J. (1994). "The politics of school violence." *Public Interest,* 116: 34-56.

Wade, T.J. & A. Brannigan. (1998). "The genesis of adolescent risk-taking: Pathways through family, school, and peers." *Canadian Journal of Sociology*, 23:1-19.

Walker, H. M., G. Colvin, & E. Ramsey. (1995). *Antisocial behavior in school: Strategies and best practices*. Pacific Grove, CA: Brooks/Cole.

Warr, M. & M. Stafford. (1991). "The influence of delinquent peers: What they think or what they do?" *Criminology*, 4:851-866.

Wiatrowski, M. & K. Anderson. (1987). "The Dimensionality of the Social Bond." *Journal of Quantitative Criminology* 3: 65-73.

Wiatrowski, M., S. Hansell, C. Massey, & D. Wilson. (1982). "Curriculum Tracking and Delinquency." *American Sociological Review* 46: 525-41.

Wilson, W.J. (1996). *When Work Disappears: The World of the New Urban Poor*. Chicago, IL: Vintage Press.

Williams, S. & R. McGee. (1991). "Adolescents self-perceptions of their strengths." *Journal of Youth and Adolescence*, 20: 325-337.

Zhang, L. & S.F. Messner. (1996). "School attachment and official delinquency status in the People's Republic of China." *Sociological Forum*, 11: 285-303.

Index